"Growth sounds so enticing until you get stalled by attitudes and bel[...]
The Growth Mindset Workbook teaches you to observe your persona[...]
strategies that can sustain your progress. If you are serious about improving your work or persona[...]
engaging book shows you how to bring a growth mindset into your daily life with practical and life-changing effects."

> —**Christine A. Padesky, PhD**, coauthor of *Mind Over Mood*
> and *The Clinician's Guide to CBT Using Mind Over Mood*

"Parallel lines of rigorous psychological research—cognitive behavioral therapy (CBT) and mindset research—have documented how we can improve our well-being, life satisfaction, and happiness. In *The Growth Mindset Workbook*, Elaine Elliott-Moskwa brilliantly describes how to effectively use the proven strategies of CBT to establish a growth mindset. By following Elliott-Moskwa's step-by-step program, the reader will learn to identify and overcome barriers to a growth mindset, and master proven CBT strategies to lead a more meaningful and fulfilled life."

> —**Dennis Greenberger, PhD**, coauthor of *Mind Over Mood*,
> and director of the Anxiety and Depression Center in Newport Beach, CA

"*The Growth Mindset Workbook* is a book that can change your life. How often have you thought, 'I can't do that'? Elaine Elliott-Moskwa provides us with powerful, practical tools to identify your biases about change, and tools that help you overcome obstacles. Highly readable, informative, and immediately useful, you will find that these ideas and techniques can help you in almost any area of your life. This is a detailed plan for 'Yes, I can' thinking."

> —**Robert L. Leahy, PhD**, director of the American Institute for Cognitive Therapy,
> and author of *If Only…: Finding Freedom from Regret*

"Elaine Elliott-Moskwa has written a superb workbook that can transform your mind and change your life. Her approach is based on a simple and powerful idea: your mindset has an enormous influence on your mental health. As an expert clinician and one of the foremost scholars in this field, Elliott-Moskwa created a masterful workbook. I highly recommend it."

> —**Stefan G. Hofmann, PhD**, Alexander von Humboldt Professor at
> Philipps-University of Marburg in Germany, and coauthor of *Learning Process-Based Therapy*

"What is a self-help book about if it's not about growth, and growth begins—according to Elaine Elliott-Moskwa—with a growth mindset. In *The Growth Mindset Workbook*, Elliott-Moskwa, an authority on the topic, presents a host of CBT skills to cultivate and nurture a new growth-oriented mindset. If you're stuck, stagnant, or paralyzed; if you're anxious, sad, or suffering; pick up this book, learn these skills, and grow."

—**Michael A. Tompkins, PhD, ABPP**, codirector of the San Francisco Bay Area
Center for Cognitive Therapy, and author of *The Anxiety and Depression Workbook*
and *Anxiety and Avoidance*

"Elaine Elliott-Moskwa has delivered an interesting and exceptional workbook to help the reader move from a fixed to a growth mindset, a go-to tool for everyone. Weaving her personal story along with relatable, professional, and everyday life examples of others, the reader is systematically helped to shift their mindset, remove the barriers to goal achievement, and build resilience and success."

—**Leslie Sokol, PhD**, president elect of the International Association of Cognitive Behavioral
Therapy (IACBT); fellow of the Association for Behavioral and Cognitive Therapies (ABCT);
distinguished founding fellow of the Academy of Cognitive and Behavioral Therapies (A-CBT);
and coauthor of *The Comprehensive Clinician's Guide to Cognitive Behavioral Therapy*

"Elaine Elliott-Moskwa takes her work on resilience to write a compelling, must-read book on how to transform a fixed mindset into a growth mindset. By showing us that a fixed mindset is a habit, she helps us learn that we can develop a growth mindset. Replete with examples, *The Growth Mindset Workbook* is an excellent resource for us to learn how to welcome challenges and convert them into successes."

—**Lata K. McGinn, PhD**, professor of psychology at Yeshiva University, cofounder of
Cognitive and Behavioral Consultants, and coauthor of *Treatment Plans and Interventions
for Depression and Anxiety Disorders* and *Treatment of OCD*

"Elaine Elliott-Moskwa has done a masterful job of practically presenting a growth mindset. Readers are led through exercises to get themselves unstuck from seeing challenges as fixed and insurmountable. The growth mindset has been embraced by schools and corporations. She applies this perspective in a personal and specific way. By basing her working in CBT, Elliot-Moskwa harnesses the power of science to help the reader enhance their potential."

—**Lynn McFarr, PhD**, professor at the University of California, Los Angeles (UCLA);
president of the IACBT; and founder of CBT California

THE
GROWTH
MINDSET
WORK BOOK

CBT Skills to Help You
Build Resilience, Increase Confidence
& Thrive through Life's Challenges

ELAINE ELLIOTT-MOSKWA, PhD

New Harbinger Publications, Inc.

Publisher's Note

This publication is designed to provide accurate and authoritative information in regard to the subject matter covered. It is sold with the understanding that the publisher is not engaged in rendering psychological, financial, legal, or other professional services. If expert assistance or counseling is needed, the services of a competent professional should be sought.

NEW HARBINGER PUBLICATIONS is a registered trademark of New Harbinger Publications, Inc.

Distributed in Canada by Raincoast Books

Cover design by Amy Daniel

Acquired by Ryan Buresh

Edited by Brady Kahn

Library of Congress Cataloging-in-Publication Data

Names: Elliott-Moskwa, Elaine S., author.
Title: The growth mindset workbook / Elaine S. Elliott-Moskwa.
Description: Oakland, CA : New Harbinger Publications, Inc., [2022] | Includes bibliographical references.
Identifiers: LCCN 2021050784 | ISBN 9781684038299 (trade paperback)
Subjects: LCSH: Belief and doubt. | Motivation (Psychology) | Self-perception. | Success--Psychological aspects. | Cognitive therapy.
Classification: LCC BF773 .E555 2022 | DDC 153.8--dc23/eng/20220103
LC record available at https://lccn.loc.gov/2021050784

Printed in the United States of America

25   24   23

10   9   8   7   6   5   4   3   2

Contents

Foreword   v

Introduction   1

Part 1: Developing a Growth Mindset

Chapter 1   Is a Fixed Mindset Holding You Back?   5

Chapter 2   What Can a Growth Mindset Do for You?   19

Chapter 3   How to Replace a Fixed Mindset with a Growth Mindset   31

Chapter 4   How to Deal with Fixed Mindset Emotions   63

Chapter 5   A Growth Mindset Action Plan to Resist Fixed Mindset   81

Chapter 6   A Growth Mindset Chart to Keep You on Track   115

Part 2: Applying a Growth Mindset

Chapter 7   A Growth Mindset to Promote Professional Goals   139

Chapter 8   A Growth Mindset for Everyday Life   165

Conclusion: How to Keep a Growth Mindset When the Going Gets Tough   187

Acknowledgments   191

References   193

Foreword

Elaine Elliott-Moskwa was one of my first PhD students ever, and was among the finest ever. She did amazing research on how people's goals could foster persistence and resilience—or the opposite. She found, for example, that people who focused on the goal of learning something new and challenging tended to be more resilient in the face of failure. But those who, instead, worried about measuring and validating their ability were more vulnerable to distress and "helplessness" when they encountered setbacks.

Her groundbreaking doctoral research set the stage for the discovery of people's self-theories or "mindsets"—that is, a fixed mindset in which people believe their personal qualities, such as their intelligence, are just fixed and cannot be developed, versus a growth mindset in which people believe that through hard work, good strategies, and help from others, they can grow their abilities.

Dr. Elliott-Moskwa then trained as a postdoctoral fellow at the University of Pennsylvania Center for Cognitive Therapy with Aaron T. Beck, the founder of cognitive behavioral therapy (CBT). And she was hooked! From there, she went on to have an illustrious career, practicing CBT for over thirty years. She established a cognitive therapy fellowship program at Harvard Medical School/Massachusetts General Hospital and is president of the Academy of Cognitive and Behavioral Therapies.

Meanwhile, decades of research documented the ways in which a growth mindset could help people thrive in terms of both their achievement and well-being. And all along the way, Dr. Elliott-Moskwa has been the bridge between this research on mindsets and the practice of CBT.

Now she has written this trailblazing book—the best I've seen—on how people can bring the two together in their own lives. That is, how people can bring an understanding of mindsets into their lives to help create the change they are seeking and reach the short- and long-term goals they are trying to achieve. Frankly, I was riveted by her fascinating case studies of people operating in the different mindsets, and inspired by the way she led the reader to see the mindsets in themselves. Finally, she provides a step-by-step program for viewing life through a new lens—that of a growth mindset—and shows how this not only can empower people to take on challenges but can guide them to act in more constructive and effective ways.

I highly recommend this book to you. It could change your life.

—Carol S. Dweck, PhD
Author of *Mindset*

Introduction

What happened to me as I wrote this book happens to others as they stretch to pursue something significant to them. I wished to make a contribution to help people flourish through life's challenges. I had never written a book, but I had the plan, a cognitive behavioral therapy (CBT) workbook to keep a growth mindset despite life's expected obstacles; the training, mentored by leading experts in the field; and the experience, my research and application of these concepts to my clients. Whatever could get in the way? A fixed mindset.

Writing this book was difficult. I had to stretch myself—apply my skills in a different way and learn new ones. Progress at times was slow. I made errors, received criticism and rejection, and heard about the successes of colleagues. The inevitable disheartening situations you face as you pursue what is important to you, be it a career, relationships, or physical or emotional health, can trigger the fixed mindset and impede your progress. The fixed mindset is not a pathology; it's an insidious, unhelpful habit. The fixed mindset is not just believing your ability is low. People who believe their ability is high can be shackled by a fixed mindset. It's your conception or view of your ability that determines how you deal with expected challenges when you reach for what you value.

The fixed mindset belief is that you have a certain amount of an ability or attribute—perhaps high, perhaps low—and that there is little that you can do to change this. The growth mindset belief is that although you may start with a particular level of ability or attribute, you can increase your ability or develop your attribute. With a growth mindset, you take on more challenges, are more resilient in the face of difficulty (adapting and learning from mistakes), and use others as mentors or resources to develop in ways that you value. With the fixed mindset, you are always worried about fixed abilities and attributes. *Am I smart? Am I talented? Am I likable? Am I a loser?* You arrange your world to avoid any unwanted answers to these questions. So you choose safe or easy tasks, run from setbacks, and avoid asking for help from others lest you seem to have deficiencies.

Even though I typically maintained a growth mindset, at times as I was writing this book, I would be caught up unaware in a fixed mindset. Whenever that happened, however, the strategies described in this very book allowed me to recognize the telltale signs of the fixed mindset and shift back to a growth mindset to complete the project.

Why write this self-help workbook on the growth mindset? Much has already been written about the importance of your mindset, but understanding the importance of a growth mindset does not mean you can easily sustain it, just as understanding that it would be better to have more positive, rational thoughts, eat healthfully, and exercise doesn't mean you will do this. It would be fabulous if you could understand that the fixed mindset can stifle your potential and then, having understood that concept, simply shift to a growth mindset and reap all the benefits and succeed.

The fixed mindset is an unhelpful habit that gets in the way of tackling life's challenges. Recognizing when you are trapped in a fixed mindset and then shifting into a growth mindset can be difficult. How, for example, do you develop a growth mindset and move on with life when you are stuck unaware in a fixed mindset (*I'm unlovable*) after the devastating end of a relationship? How do you move forward with a growth mindset and push ahead when you are mired in a fixed mindset (*I'm not talented*) after being rejected for a job you really wanted?

So how do you take an intellectual understanding of the importance of mindset and apply it in your own life? This book offers systematic steps to identify and escape from a fixed mindset and get back on track with a growth mindset. You will learn how to use certain cognitive behavioral tools to move forward with a growth mindset when you become stalled in a fixed mindset pothole somewhere on the road to your goals. In addition, there are also a host of materials available for download at the website for this book: http://www.newharbinger.com/48299.

Although much has been written for promoting the growth mindset in prekindergarten through secondary school students, little of quality has been created for adults using the evidence-based tools of CBT. What's more, rather than providing evidence-based guidance for changing fixed mindset, some authors simply tout the importance of changing it.

This book is intended for anyone searching for strategies to tackle their fixed mindset and sustain a growth mindset as well as for readers of *Mindset* (Dweck 2006). This book is also intended for mental health care professionals, managers, coaches, parents, and educators who could use the techniques to help their patients, employees, clients, children, and students maintain a growth mindset despite fixed mindset challenges.

Why should this book be written by me? The author of *Mindset*, Carol S. Dweck, PhD, was my mentor in graduate school and supervised my postdoctoral work at the Harvard School of Education, Laboratory of Human Development. My dissertation was published in a leading academic journal and has been cited over five thousand times. Later, I published papers and chapters with Dweck concerning applications of mindsets. My mentor also was Aaron T. Beck, MD, considered the father of cognitive therapy, with whom I trained at the Center for Cognitive Therapy at the University of Pennsylvania. Furthermore, I served as a consultant to David Burns, MD, author of *Feeling Good: The New Mood Therapy*, during his tenure at Penn's Presbyterian Hospital, and I helped to establish the cognitive therapy training program at the Harvard Medical School/Massachusetts General Hospital.

Currently, I am president of the Academy of Cognitive and Behavioral Therapies, the premier certifying organization for cognitive therapy. In my private practice in Princeton, I employ the cognitive behavioral self-help strategies offered in this book. Here I have aspired to bridge the academic and the clinical world and translate Dweck's book and body of research into a self-help workbook rooted in evidence-based techniques. I bring twenty-plus years of helping people shift from a fixed to a growth mindset in cherished realms in which they are not living up to their potential. I have seen its power to transform lives. It has transformed and continues to transform my own.

PART 1

Developing a Growth Mindset

CHAPTER 1

Is a Fixed Mindset Holding You Back?

Imagine two graduate students seeking employment at a research company. They work in the same field of study, microbiology, and have the same number of research publications; both have had average to above average grades in their graduate programs, and both have made some progress toward completing their PhD thesis. In other words, they have equivalent levels of skill and experience in microbiology. Imagine each being invited to do a daylong interview at the company, which includes a presentation of their research with a question-and-answer session, followed by five forty-minute interviews with potential supervisors and colleagues at the company. The interview is two weeks off.

Jim begins to prepare his presentation two weeks out. He makes some progress, but he keeps judging himself. As he prepares his talk, he begins to think, *What if I don't look impressive? What if I haven't accomplished enough in graduate school?* He pushes past this anxiety and continues to write his talk. However, he continues to be a bit distracted. He imagines being rejected for the job. He thinks about how he will be seen by those in his department if he fails to be hired. He convinces himself, *My advisors will think I was a bad choice, a lemon.* He works obsessively on the talk, saying to himself, *This is my one shot. I have to be perfect. If this doesn't work out, it will be months of searching for another opportunity, if I can find one at all.* He neglects his other departmental responsibilities and exhausts himself working on the presentation.

While working, Jim encounters two other graduate students who were recently hired, one by the same company. He feels self-conscious, saying to himself, *What will they think of me if I am not offered a position? They'll view my work as insignificant.* Because Jim's view of himself and his work are on the line, the night before the interview he has difficulty sleeping. Lying awake, he worries that, sleep deprived, he will not be able to answer questions and will be at a loss for words during the coming interview. He questions whether he should have aimed lower in his job search and even thinks about calling human resources and canceling, telling them that he is ill.

Now let's contrast this to Rob. Remember Rob and Jim have equivalent levels of skills and experience in microbiology. Let's take a look at Rob two weeks out from the interview. He, too, begins working immediately on his presentation. It is not easy, and sometimes he feels a bit frustrated, but then he says to himself, *It's important that I communicate well in my talk, and given the complexity of my topic, this will not be an easy task. How do I connect clearly with a mixed audience, some of whom may not be familiar with my research?* He spends a fair amount of time reorganizing his talk and then sets up an appointment with one of his advisors to see if he can get some input. He sees one of his peers who was recently hired by the same company and solicits her perspective on the process as well. He asks her what types of questions were asked during the interview and what was most surprising about the process. He asks her about the company itself. Although he thinks that he would like this job, he realizes that the process of interviewing will give him a window into what the culture of the company is like and whether or not it seems a match for him.

Later, as the interview approaches, he acknowledges to himself that he may not get the job offer, yet he also sees the interviewing process as a chance to learn something about this type of company and a chance to grow more comfortable during interviews. If he is not hired, he tells himself, he will need to put more effort into finding other job leads and possibly network with some alums of his graduate program. The night before the interview, Rob feels nervous but also excited. He rehearses his talk a bit and then relaxes with a movie on his computer and gets to sleep at a reasonable time. He feels prepared and recognizes that it is not possible to anticipate every question.

How is it that Jim and Rob, with equal skills and experiences, respond so very differently to the same challenging job interview? How is it that Jim's anxiety builds to a point that he loses sleep and even considers aborting the interview? How is it that Jim and Rob view their advisors and peers so differently? How is it that Jim and Rob tackle the task of preparing for their talk so differently? How do you think each of them will respond to difficulty during the actual interview? How will each of them respond to a momentary lapse during their presentations? If not hired, how will this affect the outlook of each?

Here's another example.

Jessica and Gail both got married in their twenties and put their careers on hold to be stay-at-home moms and to support their husband's careers. Now they are in their fifties and their children are in college. Both receive some surprising news from their husband—he has found someone else and would like a divorce.

Jessica feels devastated. She thinks, *How could he do this to me after all I've given him?* She feels intensely jealous of her husband's new girlfriend and deeply humiliated by the rejection. In fact, she withdraws from friends and activities, thinking that others will view her with scorn or pity. She believes that overnight she has gone from being a winner to being a loser, from being lovable to unlovable.

After a while, Jessica reconnects with a few friends, spending most of her time with them running her ex down and seeking their agreement with her venomous barbs. She now spends all her energy thinking about how to get revenge. He reduced her to nothing, and he's not going to just walk away and live happily ever after. She decides not to return to her career so that she can get the maximum amount of alimony from her ex. She tries to turn the children against their father—images of them spending time with the happy couple are intolerable. As months pass, she decides that men aren't worth the effort and that she never wants to be in another relationship. But underneath it all, she begins to doubt her attractiveness and whether or not she is truly a loser.

Now let's turn to Gail, who like Jessica receives the same shocking news. Gail is also devastated, hurt, and confused. Who wouldn't be? It takes her months to accept that her husband has chosen to leave her for another woman.

But Gail reaches out to friends. She shares the difficulty of adjusting to her newly single life but doesn't dwell on it. She makes an effort to spend time with them doing mutually enjoyable activities. She solicits the input of divorced friends who appear to have coped well. She realizes that her status as a single woman may change her relationship with some in the community, and yet she attempts to stay active, reaching out to new acquaintances.

During the divorce proceedings, her goal is to achieve a just and yet amicable separation. Although hurt, she allows that her adult children have a separate relationship with their father. As time passes, she does a bit of an assessment as to what happened in her marriage and what she would like in a future relationship. She's not sure if she wants another relationship but leaves the door open. She also starts thinking about whether she would like to reenter her career and, if so, what might be some first steps to take. She consults with some past colleagues and does some research. She sometimes feels anxious and insecure, but she also starts to see the many possibilities that lie before her.

How is it that Jessica and Gail respond so differently to such an unexpected and unwelcome event? How is it that Jessica is so mired in negative emotions like anger and jealousy whereas Gail, although hurt, seems to move on? Both are responding to objectively the same situation—a difficult divorce. How is it that their relationships with others take a different trajectory? How is it that they behave so differently with acquaintances, friends, and family?

In these two examples, people with similar skills and in similar situations respond very differently to life challenges. Whether that challenge is work-related or personal, we can see two distinctive reactions in their thoughts, emotions, and actions. Although the people in the examples are fictional, they are composites of individuals with whom I have worked during the last thirty years. I have spent years studying these responses to assist people to be resilient and successful in the face of life's challenges and setbacks.

The Importance of Mindset

In her book *Mindset: The New Psychology of Success*, Carol Dweck (2006) documents people in all walks of life who exhibit these clearly distinct patterns. She describes two different beliefs or mindsets that people hold about their abilities and attributes, and shows how these mindsets can have powerful effects on their success—in achievement fields such as school, business, science, and sports, but also in interpersonal spheres, such as forming and maintaining close relationships.

The *fixed mindset* is the belief that you have a certain amount of an ability or attribute—perhaps high, perhaps low—and that there is little that you can do to change this (Bandura and Dweck 1985). The *growth mindset* is the belief that although you may start with a particular level of ability or attribute, you can increase your ability or develop your attribute. My early work with Dweck helped lay the foundation of the growth and fixed mindset. It underlined the importance of *learning* versus *performance goals* (get better versus look-good goals) in determining whether individuals embrace challenges and withstand negative feedback, and perform at their best despite obstacles (Elliott and Dweck 1988). Later, Dweck and others demonstrated that your mindset impacted these goals (Robins and Pals 2002; Blackwell, Trzesniewski, and Dweck 2007; Mangels et al. 2006). Research showed that when people are in a growth mindset, they take on more challenges (Mueller and Dweck 1998; Beer 2002; Kray and Haselhuhn 2007). They are also more resilient in the face of difficulty (Wood and Bandura 1989). They adapt and learn from mistakes (Blackwell, Trzesniewski, and Dweck 2007; Mueller and Dweck 1998; Kammrath and Dweck 2006). And they use other people as mentors or resources to develop their abilities or attributes (Hong et al. 1999; Nussbaum and Dweck 2008).

In the fixed mindset, people are always worried about their fixed abilities and attributes. Am I smart? Am I talented? Am I likable? Am I a loser? They arrange their worlds to avoid any unwanted answers to these questions, so they choose safe or easy tasks, run from setbacks, and avoid asking for help from others, lest they seem to exhibit deficiencies.

A fixed mindset is a nightmare of driving through a remote desert toward a distant endpoint with a fuel gage that's not working. You ask, *How much fuel do I really have? Do I have enough to make it to my destination? How far do I push it? What if I run out of gas? I think I have enough to get to my destination, but what if I don't? Should I even try, or should I just pull to the side of the road?* You feel intense anxiety and fear. You feel that your survival is on the line.

Research has shown some people have more of a fixed mindset, and others have more of a growth mindset (Robins and Pals 2002). But importantly, research has also shown that a growth mindset can be learned, causing shifts in how you think, feel, and act (Nussbaum and Dweck 2008; Aronson, Fried, and Good 2002; Good, Aronson, and Inzlicht 2003; Blackwell, Trzeniewski, and Dweck 2007; Hong et al. 1999).

How This Book Can Help

You may be reading this book because you appreciate the importance of a growth mindset. Perhaps you already have a growth mindset and want to learn how to apply it more effectively or consistently. Perhaps you have read Dweck's *Mindset* and had an *Aha!* experience. You immediately recognized areas in your life where you had a fixed mindset, and you were quickly able to make the shift to a growth mindset. That's wonderful. Alternatively, perhaps you have already worked hard on developing a growth mindset to stretch the way you think and operate—and you want to stretch more.

A growth mindset can be a powerful tool to weather the challenges of life and to excel in many areas. But while the concept is simple—it's good to shift to a growth mindset when you find yourself mired in a fixed mindset—it's not that easy to do. One problem is that fixed mindsets are sometimes hard to recognize. And even when you recognize that you are stuck in a fixed mindset, making the shift may not be that easy, even when you see the advantages. Just because you have an intellectual understanding of something doesn't mean it's easy to execute change. Say, for example, you're a pitcher and want to improve your curve ball. Your coach tells you that you need to shorten your stride, change the angle of your elbow, and change your grip. You watch as your coach shows you exactly what to do. You can see what you need to do differently, but executing may be another thing. It is especially difficult because you have a habitual way of throwing a curve ball. You have to engage in deliberate practice for many hours to come up with this new way of doing things. So understanding a curve ball does not equal change. Understanding a fixed versus a growth mindset does not equal change.

Shifting from a fixed mindset to growth mindset is not just a matter of many hours of practice, either—it is a lifelong project. Even when you start out with a growth mindset to improve your skills or attributes, there are fixed mindset obstacles. There are situations that can throw you off track and into a fixed mindset. For example, you can become ill and stop viewing life in terms of growth and improvement. A negative evaluation can make you wonder about your abilities. A major mistake can make you feel unable to move forward with something that is important to you. Word that someone you know has accomplished something that you had hoped for in your life may leave you discouraged. Or, you might suddenly find pockets of fixed mindset you didn't know were there—that is, a fixed mindset might have been controlling your thoughts, feelings, and behaviors, but you didn't know it.

I've been studying mindset for years and what surprises me is that I still catch myself falling into a fixed mindset. Although I had done research with Carol Dweck, had trained with Aaron T. Beck in CBT, and had been applying CBT for twenty years to help my clients shift from a fixed to a growth mindset, my own fixed mindset almost sabotaged this book.

I want to share that experience to help you look at how fixed mindset could be preventing growth in your own life. But I need to go back to the very beginning. Carol Dweck had approached me to coauthor a chapter in an academic book (Dweck and Elliott-Moskwa 2010), and later she agreed to cowrite an article for a journal discussing applications of mindset research for CBT. I thought I was excited about writing this article. I constructed the outline and submitted a proposal to the journal, and the editor responded positively. But then I procrastinated. I felt a bit bored. It was odd—I thought that I should be committed to this project, yet I found every opportunity to avoid it, and finally abandoned it altogether. But the guilt about not writing continued to hang over my head. I tried to motivate myself by saying *I should finish this article. What's wrong with me?*

Many months later, my sister, an elementary school teacher, phoned to say that she was trying to apply the principles of *Mindset* in her classroom. I recalled a fellow psychologist who shared her struggle in using mindset with their clients. Then I remembered my own clients who wanted to read and learn more about mindset. That night, I had an epiphany. I would write a how-to manual using CBT to build on *Mindset,* so people could learn some practical and effective tools to sustain a growth mindset. I felt super excited and energized. The next morning, I began jotting down ideas, many jumbled and incomplete. I wrote throughout the day and over the next few days, sometimes on my computer and sometimes on whatever was available, like the backs of envelopes. I wrote whenever I got the chance, between patients during office hours and over lunch. I even pulled over the car while driving back from my office to capture ideas. The next day I emailed Carol to say that instead of writing a piece for an academic journal, I would work on a book for more general audiences. At its foundation would be the academic research underlying mindset theory and CBT, but the objective of the book would be to make it widely accessible with practical tools for change.

Carol responded enthusiastically. During the next few days and weeks I was amazingly motivated; I wrote an outline and an eight-page draft despite my usual load of patient appointments. I was determined and focused and filled with excitement. What a total shift in my attitude and actions! I was in a growth mindset—immersing myself in this new undertaking—plunging into the ideas even though they were not perfectly developed. Such a contrast to how I had felt and acted when I worked on the journal article. When I compared this to how I had reacted to writing the journal article, I recognized that I had been caught up in a fixed mindset at the time.

What were some of the clues that I had fallen into a fixed mindset? I automatically chose submission to an academic journal; it felt easy and safe but boring. I knew how to write articles and chapters for academic audiences; I was good at it. I would again demonstrate to my peers (and myself) that I was an academic researcher and thinker who should be taken seriously. It felt less difficult but also less interesting to me than writing this book. Once I committed to the riskier goal of writing this workbook, I felt incredibly energized. It was an opportunity to learn something different and improve as a psychologist and a writer.

But this was only the start of my journey. It would be the first of a number of encounters with fixed mindset. I did not sustain a growth mindset throughout my writing of this manual. Even though I had studied this process for years, I'd find myself mired in fixed-mindset thoughts, feelings, and actions. Then after recognizing them, I would shift to the growth mindset using my CBT tools—the same ones you will learn in this book.

A sampling of my thoughts during this process give more clues to fixed-mindset thinking:

Do I have what it takes?

What will my mentor Dr. Beck think of me if I'm not writing an academic article?

Many of my colleagues have written not one but many books! I'm way behind!

What if I am successful and have to face someone like Colbert!

What if the book is not good enough? It needs to be perfect!

It will take too much time and be too difficult. I need time to do other things I enjoy.

What if I write a book and it's never published?

What if it's published and no one reads it?

What if critics shoot it down?

What if it's full of errors?

Who am I to write a book?

What if the world is watching? What if the world doesn't care?

Along with these thoughts were fixed-mindset emotions and actions. For example, prior to sitting down at the computer to write, I would feel uneasy and tense and then engage in activities unrelated to writing a book, checking email, checking the weather forecast, finding the very best airfare for a vacation to New Orleans, submitting captions to the *New Yorker* cartoon contest. Sometimes I would be writing furiously and then get stuck in a section of the book, feel frustrated that I was not making enough progress, and procrastinate for weeks on end with other things on my to-do list, like organizing my office and shredding old files, productive things but not in keeping with my priority of writing a book. Later in the process, I would consider sending my book out to friends and colleagues for comments, feel apprehensive, and tell myself, not yet. I would delay submitting the proposal to publishers for months, worried that it wasn't perfect. My point is, even though I was committed to writing this book, it wasn't like smoothly heading down the road with a growth mindset happily ever after.

Now I'd like you to reflect on some of the trials that you have faced in your life as you tried to grow or stretch yourself. This will help you become accustomed to observing your responses to these challenges.

Is a Fixed Mindset Getting in Your Way?

Let's investigate how a fixed mindset may be preventing you from pursuing your valued goals. Think back to a time when you were dissatisfied with some aspect of your life—maybe it was about school or work, your relationships, or yourself—and you tried to make a change and stretch yourself. Perhaps you applied for a challenging but interesting job, or you took a risk with a new and exciting relationship. Now consider that moment in time where you hit a roadblock in your pursuit. For example, you received an email rejection after the job interview, or your new heartthrob announces they would like to be friends after a few months together. Everyone has these experiences. Reflect back on that moment when you were striving for something that was important and you experienced a roadblock. Flash back to the point of that setback, when you had hoped to improve your life in a way that was significant to you. What had you hoped for? What was happening? Who was there? What did you feel, think, do at that moment? Use the exercise below to get better at observing your responses to these expected life challenges.

Answer the questions in the space provided to explore how a fixed mindset may be preventing you from pursuing your goals.

1.   Have you ever found yourself bored or dissatisfied with some aspect of your life: your work, your relationships, or yourself? Describe the circumstance.

_____

_____

2.   At that time, did you challenge yourself to do something new and more interesting and that might stretch you but that made you feel a bit apprehensive? If so, what did you try? What were your thoughts and feelings as you tackled this activity that might have allowed you to grow or change in ways that were important to you?

_____

_____

3.   Did you find yourself getting off track or avoiding the challenge, even though you valued improving? That is, what roadblocks did you encounter as you tried to extend yourself or grow? Close your eyes and try to picture them. Try to describe this, using the next series of questions as a guide.

Were you concerned about being judged and, if so, by whom?

_____

Did someone you care about or respect criticize you? What did they say? Did they say anything helpful? How did you feel? How did you respond?

_____

_____

_____

_____

Were you concerned you wouldn't be good enough?

_____

Did you make mistakes? If so, what were the mistakes? What were your feelings and thoughts about the mistake? What actions did you take afterward?

_____

_____

_____

_____

Did you question the effort you put in, even though you were doing something you truly valued? Were you concerned it should be easier, like it was for others? Who were those others?

_____

_____

_____

Did you compare yourself to someone who seemed to be doing a better job of achieving what you wanted? To whom did you compare yourself?

_____

_____

Did you stop and think about your progress? What were your thoughts? How did you feel about your progress? What was going on?

_____

_____

_____

4. If you passed up something new even though it seemed interesting and potentially broaden-
    ing, what happened?

    _____

    _____

    Did some emotions get in the way? What were those emotions?

    _____

    Did you think about what a struggle it might be or how difficult it might be? What did you feel
    and say to yourself about the struggle?

    _____

    Were you concerned about the competition—that others were better? Who were those
    others?

    _____

    Were you concerned you would be judged by others? Who would have judged you? What
    might they think about you? What did you feel when you considered their possible judgment?

    _____

    _____

    _____

    Were you concerned that you wouldn't live up to your own standard? What was your standard?

    _____

    Were you concerned about making errors? What were they?

    _____

5. Alternatively, despite roadblocks, were you able to move forward? Try to picture what
    happened.

    How did you encourage yourself?

    _____

How did you overcome any negative emotions?

_____

Did you look to others for support? Who supported you? What did they say or do to help?

_____

_____

_____

How did you grapple with your mistakes?

_____

How did you deal with your comparison with others?

_____

How did you cope with criticism?

_____

Remember, almost everyone has fixed mindset responses when they are moving toward a life they value. And even if your path has been strewn with roadblocks, have no fear. What's key is that you recognize fixed-mindset responses. This book will help you do that, and it will give you the tools to get back on track with your growth mindset and move forward.

How to Use This Book

This workbook is your how-to manual for shifting mindsets. I will be your coach as you learn how to spot when a fixed mindset is getting in your way and how to tackle it and shift to a growth mindset. Strategies and techniques pioneered by Aaron T. Beck (Beck 1976; Beck, Rush, Shaw, and Emery 1979) plus other evidence-based cognitive and behavioral techniques (Young, Klosko, and Weishaar 2003; Persons and Tompkins 2007; Hayes and Lillis 2012; Hofmann et al. 2010; Kaplan and Tolin 2011; Leahy, Tirch, and Napolitano 2011) have been specially modified for use in shifting mindsets.

A fixed mindset is like a habit that's automatically triggered in certain situations. For example, some people have a habit of smoking when they are in social situations with fellow smokers. At a party, they feel an urge to smoke, think *I need a cigarette,* and pull the pack from their pocket. Like the party for the smoker, certain situations set off the fixed mindset with self-limiting thoughts, feelings, and actions. Although you may feel okay and not at all terrible, the fixed-mindset habit is sabotaging you and preventing you from developing in ways that are important to you. CBT exercises in this book will help you identify your habitual fixed mindset and shift back to growth-enhancing thoughts, feelings, and actions.

Why do I use CBT? It's not because a fixed mindset is a pathology or because it necessarily requires therapy. CBT has improved the lives of people with serious disorders like depression, panic, and even schizophrenia (Leahy 2004; Hofmann et al. 2012). But you do not need to be seriously troubled to benefit from CBT principles and strategies. I use them because they are powerful and proven ways to make changes that are important for you.

This workbook will give you a CBT toolbox to propel you out of a fixed-mindset pothole when you are stuck somewhere on your adventure to develop your skills and attributes. It will take practice and effort to use these tools effectively, and at points during this process you might be tempted to say, "Forget it. This is too difficult. I'm turning back and will just stay where I am." But with this road map and your CBT tools, you'll pursue the goals you value, even if there is a risk of looking foolish or incompetent as you persevere. You'll view setbacks as expected and as opportunities for learning and growth. You'll view other people as potential resources (not judges of your underlying competence and worth), and you'll be proud of your progress, even when you haven't quite succeeded in reaching your goal.

Summary

Regardless of your abilities, two mindsets can have an astounding impact on your work, social, and personal goals and achievements.

Fixed mindset: The belief that you have a certain amount of an ability or attribute—perhaps high, perhaps low—and that there is little you can do to change this.

With the fixed mindset you:

- Avoid challenges, choose safe or easy tasks

- Run from setbacks

- Hide and worry about mistakes

- Avoid asking for help from others, lest you reveal deficiencies

Growth mindset: The belief that although you may start with a particular level of ability or attribute, you can develop your ability or attribute:

- Take on more challenges

- Become more resilient in the face of difficulty

- Adapt and learn from mistakes

- Use other people as mentors or resources

Shifting from a fixed to a growth mindset can have a huge impact on your life. But understanding the importance of growth mindset is not the same as being able to sustain it, and it can be easy to fall into old habits that get in the way of developing skills or attributes that you value.

A fixed mindset is difficult to detect, but there are common thoughts, emotions, and behaviors that signal its presence. This means you can recognize it and use CBT tools to shift back to growth. This workbook will help you sustain a growth mindset on your journey toward the life you value.

CHAPTER 2

What Can a Growth Mindset Do for You?

Having a fixed mindset can blindside you and keep you from pursuing what you value even if by most measures you would appear to be successful. The truth is that being outwardly successful does not necessarily mean that you always continue to grow or feel fulfilled. Take someone who is often in the public eye, Matthew McConaughey, who won the 2014 Academy Award for best actor in the movie *Dallas Buyers Club*. Objectively, from the perspective of his fans, McConaughey was extremely successful even before he won his Oscar. He was a popular, handsome star who'd appeared in a series of romantic comedies and had a lovely wife and two young children.

McConaughey seemed to be pursuing his valued career goals of acting and his personal goals of family. How is it that this actor who mostly played the part of a sexy, shirtless guy romping on the beach eventually won an Academy Award for portraying an emaciated, HIV-positive, homophobic cowboy? From our perspective, he took stock of his life, assessed his satisfaction in terms of his valued goals, and determined that there was another way in which he might grow in his acting career. This other way of growing his skills as an actor was risky in that he knew he was good at his roles in romantic comedy but had no proven track record for more serious roles.

In a 2014 CBS interview with Lee Cowan, McConaughey described his journey from rom-com star to Oscar winner: "What changed? I was going fine in my career, I was enjoying my career. My life started to feel more exciting than my career, which I was happy that it goes that way instead of the *other* way. But I said, I'm gonna have to stop doing what I've been doing...The first thing was saying no to the things that I was doing. I got together with my wife. We said, 'Look, we're financially okay. We're gonna eat and pay the rent. It's gonna be dry for a while. Don't know how long.' That was sort of scary. We didn't know how long. I just wanted to spice it up. I wanted to shake things up for myself. I wanted to go down to do some roles that shook my floor, that made me uncomfortable."

For two years, McConaughey declined comfortable roles. He played parts that were atypical for him: a hit man in the movie *Killer Joe*, a traveling defense attorney in *The Lincoln Lawyer*, an eccentric fugitive in *Mud*, and the owner of a strip club in *Magic Mike*.

McConaughey said that he "un-branded." He chose to pay greater attention to his experience in the moment: "I've noticed that if I stick to the process and love the process and what I'm doing, head down, but not thinking about the results—I really haven't been thinking about results for some time—it's interesting, because now more results are coming my way" (Cowan 2014). At the time of the interview, McConaughey had been nominated for the Oscar in *Dallas Buyers Club*. The script had been turned down by producers 137 times. For the role, McConaughey lost forty-seven pounds in four months.

So, we have this successful actor taking stock of what appears to be an accomplished life and then making a commitment to take a series of risks to grow his acting skills. We do not know if a fixed mindset prevented him from taking those risks earlier or if his risk-taking represents someone who typically has a growth-mindset perspective. The takeaway here is that success should be measured not by outward appearances but by how you feel about your own experiences, and this is true, no matter who you are.

To discover what a growth mindset can do for you, first you must take stock of your life, to ask yourself, how satisfied are you feeling with the different parts of your life that are important to you?

Where Do You Want to Grow?

To continue with this workbook, you need to value and be excited about your destination. How satisfied are you with the different areas of your life that are important to you? Are there areas of your life where you would like to grow, to improve, to stretch yourself and your skills?

For example, some people feel satisfied with their career but feel they would like to improve their social life; they may wish to make more friends or find an intimate partner. Others may wish to improve the relationships that they already have. On the other hand, some feel good about their social life but would like to stretch themselves in terms of their work or perhaps consider a different line of work. Others value personal changes in terms of physical or emotional health; they may want to pursue a healthier lifestyle or would like to feel less stressed.

Still others may wish to expand their horizons in the form of a new hobby or would like to do more to give back to their community.

It's not always easy to figure out where you would like to grow, stretch, or improve, especially if you have been caught up in a fixed mindset. A fixed mindset is limiting in that you restrict yourself to situations where you feel safe. For example, you may have found that it's easy to hang with your old friends from high school or college. Or, maybe you say to yourself, *Who has time for friends when I'm working sixty hours a week?* Expanding your network of friends may be a worthwhile goal, but the idea may not occur to you, because the process of putting yourself out to new people would feel uncomfortable. Or, alternatively, it may not occur to you to pursue a management position at the office, because you are good at your current job and you know what to expect. It is safe and predictable. Maybe you tell yourself, *I'm not the manager type.*

A life satisfaction questionnaire will help you define the areas of your life in which you would like to improve, and where you could benefit from a growth mindset. As you fill it out, keep in mind that you're looking for at least one area in which you would like to grow, so you can set a goal in keeping with that improvement. This growth goal doesn't have to be life altering. If you choose just one small but somewhat risky goal that stretches your skills, what you will learn as you move toward this goal will help you pursue other, larger goals in the future. That is, through the process of defining one small goal, you can practice navigating with your growth mindset and CBT tools.

There are three parts to this questionnaire, which I'll walk you through with the example of Alexandra's responses. You can download a copy of the life satisfaction questionnaire at http://www. newharbinger.com/48299.

Life Satisfaction Questionnaire

Part 1. Rate your satisfaction with different areas your life. Think about what's important to you in the areas of your social, personal, or work life.

Under each topic, rate how satisfied you feel on a scale of -3 to 3, where -3 is very dissatisfied and 3 is very satisfied (a 0 means you are neutral). Next to your rating, describe specifically what you're satisfied or dissatisfied with. If there are other important areas in your life that are not on the list, add them under "other."

Social

Friends: _____

_____

Family: _____

_____

Intimate partners: _____

_____

Community: _____

_____

Other: _____

_____

Personal

Leisure activities: _____

_____

Health: _____

_____

Physical environment (home/apartment): _____

_____

Emotional well-being: _____

_____

Finances: _____

_____

Other: _____

_____

Career/Work/Achievement

Job: _____

_____

Hobbies: _____

_____

Volunteer activities: _____

_____

Other: _____

_____

Let's use Alexandra to illustrate how to fill out part 1. Alexandra is twenty-seven, single, and working as a legal secretary in a large corporate law firm. She recently began to reflect more on what she wants from life after going through some big changes: her best friend accepted a promotion and moved to another city, her brother and his wife had their first child, and her parents moved out of state. She used the questionnaire to take a broader look at her life and examine if she might benefit from more of a growth mindset.

Alexandra's social life

Friends: *0 (neutral) Enjoy a night out with them for dinner and movies but miss my community college friends who were trying to change the world. Liked working with them on a political campaign.*

Family: *+2 (satisfied) Have a close relationship with my parents. Will miss them and keep in touch.*

Intimate partners: *-3 (very dissatisfied) Don't date much, don't have a steady relationship. Wish I did.*

Community: *+2 (satisfied) Live in an apartment complex and enjoy hanging with neighbors.*

Alexandra's personal life

Leisure activities: *+1 (somewhat satisfied) Like watching new movies and reading mystery novels.*

Health: *-1 (somewhat dissatisfied) Trying to stay healthy—eating more vegetables and less red meat and walk the stairs in the office for exercise, but healthy food isn't that tasty and walking the stairs isn't much fun.*

Physical environment: *-1 (somewhat dissatisfied) Apartment has good bones but is gloomy and dark.*

Emotional well-being: *+2 (satisfied) Generally good, no real anxiety or sadness.*

Finances: *-2 (dissatisfied) Need to manage my finances better. Make a decent salary, but can't seem to put money into savings or retirement.*

Alexandra's career/work/achievement

Job: *-3 (very dissatisfied) Been a legal secretary for three years. Just got a good review from my boss. She likes that I'm detail oriented, great at organizing and communicating. But I'm bored with the same old tasks. Enjoy my office mates.*

Hobbies: *+1 (somewhat satisfied) My cat is my hobby.*

Volunteer activities: *Not interested.*

Part 2. Identify areas where you are dissatisfied. Circle the items where your satisfaction ratings are 0 and below. Take a closer look at these areas that are important to you but where you feel dissatisfied in terms of growth or improvement. Unpack this dissatisfaction by asking yourself these questions:

- Are there activities that you think may be interesting or fun, but you have avoided out of concern for failing or looking foolish?

- Are there areas that you value and think you might be good at, but you've avoided them and avoided stretching yourself because you don't want to find out that you're not?

- Are there activities or situations that feel safe but boring? These activities may be ones where you feel confident that you can show yourself to be competent (or even talented) but perhaps you find that you're a bit weary of them? What activities may be more fun or interesting but feel a bit risky?

- Are there activities that you would like to try but were concerned that you lacked the ability?

- Are there some personal changes that you've tried to make but became frustrated and then gave up? Would you value these personal changes if you felt you could make them with little effort?

- Were there times in your life when you felt challenged and excited about learning something new? What was that activity? Can you still feel that excitement? Can you feel that excitement (along with some natural trepidations) as you contemplate something new? What were the aspects of that activity that you enjoyed? Is there a similar activity now that you may engage in?

Here are the items that Alexandra rated 0 or below along with her responses to the questions in part 2. Under "social," she circled:

Friends: *0 Considered joining a local environmental group, because I believe global warming is real and thought it might be a way to make new friends. But was hesitant—thought that I wouldn't fit in, wouldn't be taken seriously.*

Intimate partners: *–3 Tried online dating because my friend Jan met her fiancé online. After just one date, they really hit it off. I have been on three one-time dates and still no long-term relationship.*

Under "personal," Alexandra circled

Health: *-1 Just not a cook. An office friend goes to yoga classes after work. She likes yoga because it makes her feel better mentally and physically. I thought yoga might be fun but can't get myself to sign up for a class. My friend is so thin. I'd look so foolish doing an upward-facing dog pose in my old workout tights.*

Physical environment: *-1 Once I tried to fix up my entire apartment. Started by painting the bathroom blue. I thought I'd be good at it because I used to help my parents with repairs. What a mess. Color turned out to be wrong. Walls were streaky. I gave up after that. An updated apartment would be terrific, if it weren't so tough.*

Finances: *-2 I once put $50 a month into a savings account. Then I had a chance to take a cruise with friends to Jamaica. I spent all my savings account. Told myself that it would be great to have a nest egg, but it is so hard to save.*

Under "career/work/achievement," Alexandra circled:

Job: *-3 Thought about going for a paralegal certificate at night and felt excited about it, but the thought of taking courses again makes me nervous. Have been out of school too long compared to others.*

Part 3. Turn your dissatisfactions into specific growth goals. Choose an area of your life (personal, social, career/work/achievement) that is important to you but where you feel dissatisfied. Use the growth goal worksheet to turn your dissatisfaction into specific growth goals. Alexandra's worksheet responses follow as an example.

You can download a copy of this growth goal worksheet at http://www.newharbinger.com/48299.

Growth Goal Worksheet

Instructions: In the space provided under these instructions, write down a growth goal, the first small step you will take toward that goal, any feelings that make you uncomfortable with taking this step, and when you will schedule the step in your calendar. Do this for up to three different growth goals.

Growth goal: Choose an area (social, personal, or career/work/achievement) where stretching yourself would increase your satisfaction. What growth goal may excite you even though, when you consider it, you get scared, feel avoidant, and perhaps fear failing?

First small step: What first small step could you take to begin to grow or improve in this area of your life? Can you imagine or visualize taking this small step? If not, ask yourself is there another small step that you would need to take beforehand? Visualize taking this small step at a specific point in time. It needs to be a step that makes you feel moderately uncomfortable or a bit uneasy.

Even-though feeling: Describe what makes you a bit uncomfortable or uneasy about taking a small step. What exactly is making you apprehensive or uncomfortable? It may be a feeling or a thought. Commit to taking the small step despite your discomfort.

Schedule the step on your calendar: This can be a physical calendar or on your phone, wherever you are most likely to see it and take action.

1. Growth goal: _____

    First small step (visualize): _____

    Even-though feeling: _____

    Schedule step on calendar date: _____

2. Growth goal: _____

    First small step (visualize): _____

    Even-though feeling: _____

    Schedule step on calendar date: _____

3. Growth goal: _____

    First small step (visualize): _____

    Even-though feeling: _____

    Schedule step on calendar date: _____

To illustrate how to turn your dissatisfaction into a specific growth goal, here are Alexandra's responses to the worksheet:

---

1. Growth goal: *Personal, improve fitness.*

    First small step (visualize): *Sign up for yoga classes.*

    Even-though feeling: *Afraid of looking foolish*

    Schedule step on calendar: *Tomorrow at lunch*

2. Growth goal: *Career, beef up my paralegal skills by taking some night courses.*

    First small step (visualize): *Research online courses for possible options.*

    Even-though feeling: *Embarrassed if the oldest person in the class*

    Schedule step on calendar: *This weekend, Sunday morning*

3. Growth goal: *Social, expand my friend group.*

    First small step (visualize): *Attend meeting of the environmental group at the local high school.*

    Even-though feeling: *Nervous I won't fit in*

    Schedule step on calendar: *Attend meeting next Thursday night.*

Now you have identified some areas where you would like to improve and some first steps toward that improvement. Congratulations. You are well on your way!

Or maybe you haven't yet filled out the questionnaire and worksheet. If you are like many of the people with whom I've worked, you may have skipped the above exercise because it felt like too much effort. That's okay! Change does take effort. It is not too late to go back and complete your ratings and respond to the questions posed. Remember the purpose is to define an area of growth in your life that you will be excited about. These questions may be difficult—that's part of the point—but once you wrestle with them and then take your first small step, you are on the road to broadening and enriching your life.

Summary

Even people who appear very successful can be dissatisfied with some areas of their lives and profit from the growth mindset. You can use the life satisfaction questionnaire to assess your satisfaction with your personal, social, or work life, and determine where you would like to grow, to improve, and to stretch yourself and your skills. This questionnaire can be used to:

- Rate your satisfaction with different areas your life

- Identify areas where you would like to improve or grow

- Turn your dissatisfactions into specific growth goals

From here, you can schedule and begin to take that first small step toward change.

CHAPTER 3

How to Replace a Fixed Mindset with a Growth Mindset

Your journey to your growth goal is filled with potential perils—situations that precipitate a haze of fixed mindset reactions that can obscure your passage to a fulfilling life. How do you sustain a growth mindset in light of a disheartening situation? To respond more consistently with a growth mindset perspective, you need to pinpoint your fixed mindset thoughts, feelings, and actions that get in your way and generate growth mindset thoughts, feeling, and behaviors. This is essential, because understanding the growth mindset and its constellation of responses can serve as your traction or equilibrium when you fall into a fixed mindset. If you can appreciate and comprehend the distinctive patterns of the growth mindset, then you can define a constructive, beneficial alternative. In other words, when you find yourself trapped in a fixed mindset, you can begin to climb out of it by framing and building a growth mindset.

The growth mindset is an alternative framework for viewing yourself and your attributes. It is akin to entering a different universe, where your view of your abilities, mistakes, struggles, and setbacks, along with your view of other people, changes. Weirdly, you begin to see obstacles as opportunities rather than roadblocks, just like an experienced growth mindset skier or snowboarder who, upon encountering moguls (snow bumps), sees them as a chance to increase their skiing or snowboarding skills.

You will learn to be a careful observer of your thoughts, feelings, and actions when you face trying conditions, or possible obstacles in your path. You'll learn to tune into them and pick up the telltale signs of a fixed mindset and shift back into the growth mindset.

What hazardous conditions might you encounter as you pursue your growth goals? Let's look at some of the ones that Alexandra faced when she took steps to accomplish her growth goals (see her responses under the growth goal worksheet in chapter 2) and some of those that I faced in writing this book.

Alexandra:

- *During my first paralegal course exam, I blanked on the questions in one of the sections.*

- *My first yoga class was much tougher and strenuous than I imagined.*

- *After two weekends of painting my condo, I realized I was about one-quarter through the paint job.*

Me:

- *After finishing an outline of the book, I confronted the task of organizing and writing the remainder of the book.*

- *I learned of a colleague who had published his ninth self-help book.*

I think of these situations as *potholes*. Like Alexandra and me, when you are doing your best to drive toward your desired goals, bang, you will hit a pothole that can jolt you into a fixed mindset. There are six types of situations that may give rise to a fixed mindset:

1. Facing the valued but challenging task ahead

2. Experiencing the task as difficult, requiring effort

3. Evaluating your progress

4. Making mistakes

5. Encountering praise or criticism from others, especially authority figures

6. Hearing about the success or failures of others

What types of potholes did Alexandra and I face in the situations described earlier? Refer back to the bulleted list, and jot down the type after each example.

Here are the answers. Alexandra faced three different types of potholes: making mistakes, experiencing the task as effortful and difficult, and evaluating your progress. I faced two types of potholes: facing your challenging task and hearing about the success or failure of others.

What barriers do you imagine confronting or have you already confronted in moving toward your growth goals? Refer to the six types of situations that give rise to a fixed mindset as you think about your experience. Imagine confronting these situations or bring any to mind that you have already experienced. Write down two here:

_____

_____

Potholes like these in your path may set off a barrage of fixed mindset thoughts, feelings, and reactions and throw you off course. Watch out for them, just as a driver stays alert for possible hazards on the road. When seeing a ball travel across a street or a truck weaving quickly in and out of traffic, the driver becomes more focused and attentive. Like the experienced motorist, slow down when you see a growth mindset menace; pause and observe your reactions. Monitoring your responses is critical for change.

Here's another example. Suppose your growth goal is to develop in your career, and you receive a below-average performance review from your boss. What is your growth mindset challenge? Imagine getting such a review. Put yourself in that situation. See your boss's face, hear their words, and tune into your reactions. How would you respond? How would you feel? What would your thoughts be when you receive such a disappointing evaluation when you'd hoped to advance? Would you:

1. Feel angry and irritated, avoid your boss whenever possible, and think *What a moron, they have no idea how hard I work!* Then denigrate your boss to coworkers.

2. Feel embarrassed and ashamed and think, *I've failed and I'm about to lose my job!* Then avoid your boss and coworkers.

3. Feel a bit apprehensive and think, *What specifically are my weaknesses? Did my boss mention any positives? How do I improve before my next review?* Then seek out additional information from your boss and other resources for improvement.

Different people may have very different reactions. Some people may initially have a fixed mindset response (like 1 or 2) and then shift into a growth mindset response (like 3). Some people are able to make this shift fairly quickly. For others, the shift occurs much more slowly or perhaps not at all.

Six Common Fixed Mindset Thoughts and Their Antidotes

When you hit a pothole, it's best to tune into your *mindset self-talk,* or what you automatically say to yourself. Even when you have been tooling along with a growth mindset, a difficult situation may jolt you into a fixed mindset, and your self-talk in this circumstance will give you a clue as to whether or not this has happened. With a fixed mindset, you think in ways that throw you off track and hold you back. If you can identify your unhelpful fixed mindset self-talk and replace it with growth mindset thoughts, you can continue to move forward.

Again, let's consider Alexandra. She mostly had a growth mindset about her paralegal course, she looked forward to class, found the reading relevant, did the homework, and studied for her first exam. It was pretty smooth sailing. But when she took the exam, she blanked on one section. What Alexandra says to herself at this point reveals her mindset. What might she think if she has fallen into a fixed mindset?

Can you see if she thinks *I'm not cut out to be a paralegal,* this will hamper her motivation to read the required material? If she thinks *Others have aced this exam, and I don't have what it takes,* may she feel embarrassed and avoid office hours with her instructor and skip a student study group?

You can spot fixed mindset self-talk because it falls into one of these six patterns:

1. All-or-none judgment of self when you are faced with a challenging task

2. Viewing your efforts negatively when a task is difficult

3. Perfectionist standards when assessing your progress or performance

4. Magnification or minimization of your mistakes

5. Viewing others, especially authorities, as judges when you are praised or criticized

6. Competitive comparisons with peers when hearing about their successes or failures

Look back at Alexandra's self-talk when she blanks on one section of the exam. Can you spot some of the above patterns? For each of these patterns, there's an antidote of growth mindset self-talk. The following sections give examples of these fixed mindset thought patterns and growth mindset antidotes you can use in response.

1. All-or-None Judgment of Self When Facing a Challenging Task

One red flag for a fixed mindset is all-or-none (or black-and-white) thinking about yourself when you are about to engage in a valued but challenging task. If you believe that you have what it takes, then you make a totally positive judgment about yourself. If you believe that you don't have what it takes, then you make a totally negative judgment about yourself. In either case, you are operating from a fixed mindset.

Listen for all-or-nothing words when you are thinking about yourself. Don't forget that what you say to yourself may be positive or negative when you are judging yourself in this way. The following list is a sample of possible all-or-none judgments. Check off any that you may have said to yourself when you faced a challenge. Add other self-judgments you've had, starting with *I am…*

☐ *Not smart/smart*

☐ *Stupid/a genius*

☐ *Not good enough/the best*

☐ *A loser/the greatest*

☐ *Weak/strong*

- [ ] *Not important/important*

- [ ] *Irresponsible/responsible*

- [ ] *Boring/interesting*

- [ ] *Unattractive/attractive*

- [ ] *Defective/perfect*

- [ ] *A bad/a good person*

- [ ] *A coward/a hero*

- [ ] *Undeserving/special*

- [ ] *Inferior/superior*

- [ ] _____

Growth Mindset Antidote: Analysis of Current Skill or Attribute

With a growth mindset, when you are about to tackle a challenging task, your attention is not on a global judgment of yourself but on how you can develop. You make an accurate assessment of the situation and your current level of skill, so you can make a plan and take realistic steps for change. You ask yourself, *How is it going, and what may I do to move forward?* The focus is on the here and now and an immersion in the task at hand or connection with others. Remember, the growth mindset is not about unrealistic positive thinking about your skills. It is a considered analysis of your skill level, perhaps high or low. Thoughts in a fixed mindset center on global judgments of self and are embodied in the question *Am I or am I not good enough?* The growth mindset, on the other hand, is embodied in the question, *What are my skills currently, and how do I improve?* As you read through the examples below, contrasting fixed and growth mindset self-talk in the face of a challenging task, listen carefully to the pattern of global self-judgment versus skills analysis and the how-to-improve question.

Fixed mindset self-talk: A homeowner walks into his garden and sees thistle and weeds and thinks, *I am a horrible gardener. The thistle and weeds are out of control.*

Growth mindset self-talk: A homeowner walks into his garden and sees thistle and weeds and thinks, *These weeds are not attractive, and I love being out in my garden. How do I tackle this? I haven't spent much time weeding, so how can I do this more consistently? Thistle seem to be an especially difficult weed to eradicate. I'll check the internet for some possible solutions for controlling thistle.*

Note that the homeowner is realistic in his assessment. Weeds are not attractive to him, and his garden needs attention. With a growth mindset, however, the focus is not a judgment of himself as a *horrible* gardener but an analysis of how he may improve his gardening skills, as he values his garden.

Fixed mindset self-talk: A job applicant receives an email about making the cut for a second round of interviews for a position in a consulting firm that she covets. She says to herself, *Such genius! I have nailed this.*

Growth mindset self-talk: A job applicant receives an email about making the cut for a second round of interviews for a position in a consulting firm that she covets. She says to herself, *So excited! This is a great chance. I prepared well for the first interview. I researched the company to understand how my skills intersect with the requirements of the position. I came up with questions that I believe were important for me to glean whether or not the culture of this firm matched my expectations. What would make sense in preparing for this next round of interviews?*

In contrast to the applicant with the fixed mindset, who deemed herself a genius after receiving a callback, the applicant in the growth mindset is not making an all-or-none judgment of herself. She launches into specific assessments of her perceived strengths in the first interview. Although she clearly is excited about the prospect of a second interview, she is not taking for granted that she will nail it and has begun to analyze how to prepare for the next round. This example also illustrates how even a positive all-or-none judgment may have the consequence of decreasing the likelihood of skill development.

2. Viewing Your Efforts Negatively When a Task Is Difficult

The second red flag for a fixed mindset is a pattern of self-talk that negatively evaluates effort. In other words, the more you try, the less talented you are. Fixed mindset tells you that good things are supposed to come easy.

Listen carefully to your self-talk about effort. The following thoughts are indicative of this thinking pattern. Check off any thoughts that you may have had when you struggled with a task. Add any others that reflect your view of effort.

☐ *This is too hard/too difficult.*

☐ *This should be easy.*

☐ *I should be breezing through this.*

☐ *This shouldn't be such a struggle.*

☐ *Don't let them see me sweat.*

☐ _____

Growth Mindset Antidote: Viewing Your Efforts Positively When a Task Is Difficult

Growth mindset values and expects effort. Where fixed mindset thinks that greater effort equals less ability, growth mindset knows that the harder you try, the better your chance for improvement. You have to exert some effort to make progress, and your thoughts center around that expectation. Effort is anticipated and not devalued.

Fixed mindset self-talk: An architect who has spent countless hours on a recent project for an important client receives some positive feedback from his colleagues and says to himself, *It was a piece of cake.*

Growth mindset self-talk: An architect who has spent countless hours on a recent project for an important client receives some positive feedback from his colleagues and says to himself, *I spent many hours on this project, and I believe the results reflect that effort. It was not easy, but I learned a lot and stretched my design skills in the process.*

Note that the architect with a fixed mindset downplayed his efforts, as greater effort in this mindset equals less ability. The architect with a growth mindset acknowledges that the process was not easy and sees the value of the energy expended.

Fixed mindset self-talk: A father who wants to develop a closer relationship with his fourteen-year-old tries to engage him in conversation on the drive home from school. But his son doesn't even look up from his iPhone when he asks him, "How did your day go?" The father thinks, *Forget it. Why bother trying?*

Growth mindset self-talk: A father who wants to develop a closer relationship with his fourteen-year-old tries to engage him in conversation on the drive home from school. But his son doesn't even look up from his iPhone when he asks him, "How did your day go?" The father thinks, *This may not be easy. He has a habit of texting his friends when we're in the car together, and I have a habit of listening to the news station and not talking. I will continue to try to connect with him. Maybe I can ask him a more specific question like, What was the best or worst part of the day? and share a little more about my day. It's worth the effort to try harder to connect with him.*

3. Perfectionist Standards When Assessing Progress or Performance

The third red flag of a fixed mindset is thinking that uses perfectionistic all-or-nothing standards. Anything less than 100 percent is unacceptable. You do not think of your performance in shades of gray. The result is either all good or all bad, with nothing in between.

In addition, with a fixed mindset, there often is a sense of urgency about making progress toward achieving your goals. Fixed mindset says that if you are really smart, special, or superior, progress should be swift and the results perfect. There is a constant judgment of where you are and how far you have gotten. When you are evaluating your outcomes in this way, you may hear yourself using words like *enough, should,* and *must.* Check off the self-talk you have heard as you have evaluated your progress, and add other examples.

☐   *I should have done better.*

☐   *I haven't done enough.*

☐   *This isn't good enough*

☐   *This must be perfect!*

☐   *This is horrible!*

☐   *This is the best!*

☐   _____

Growth Mindset Antidote: Any-Percent-Is-Something Standard in Assessing Progress

In a fixed mindset, anything less than perfect is an indication that you don't have what's needed. In a growth mindset, skills build over time, so your standard for progress is incremental. Any improvement is acceptable, even if only slight. Although you are eager to move forward, there is not an overwhelming sense of urgency. Small steps are acknowledged as making headway. You are realistic about your performance; you accept it and analyze it for ways to improve. Your thinking revolves around the question, *What is the current level of my skill, and how do I take an incremental step to move forward?*

Fixed mindset self-talk: A student spends two days and nights studying for her biology exam. On the day of the exam, she tells herself, *I haven't studied enough.*

Growth mindset self-talk: A student spends two days and nights studying for her biology exam. On the day of the exam, she tells herself, *I have put in hours of studying for this exam. I could have studied more but chose to focus also on my history assignment. At this point, there's not much left to do but take the* *exam and do the best I can. Based on how things go, I'll consider evaluating my approach for studying for this course.*

In the first example, the student says to herself that she has not studied enough. Such a fixed mindset conclusion is done in service of determining whether or not you have enough ability or enough of a certain attribute to succeed. This judgment about her progress in studying is made in an all-or-nothing manner, where anything short of 100 percent is not enough. Yet enough is a moving target. In a growth mindset, the student attempts to make a realistic assessment of how much she has studied.

Clearly you can always study more. You could study 24/7, and yet realistically, you can only study so much. The student with a growth mindset views any percent of studying as helpful and yet tries to specifically address how she may improve her study skills in the future.

Fixed mindset self-talk: A young woman returns to her hometown for the holidays and has dinner with some extended family members. There are some silent pauses as she converses with her cousin, whom she hasn't seen since the last holiday. She thinks, *I'm not entertaining enough.*

Growth mindset self-talk: A young woman returns to her hometown for the holidays and has dinner with some extended family members. There are some silent pauses as she converses with her cousin, whom she hasn't seen since the last holiday. She thinks to herself, *I would like to reconnect with my cousin. We haven't spoken for a year, so I expect it will take a bit of time to feel comfortable. Some silences are expected, as we try to find some common ground for conversation.*

Note that the young woman within the growth mindset is aware of some awkward moments, and yet she sees these as likely to decrease as she continues to reach out to her cousin. In contrast to the fixed mindset, in which she proclaims, *I'm not entertaining enough,* in the growth mindset she sees the rebuilding of a relationship on a continuum and expects that initially progress may be slow. She sees progress in connecting with her cousin as incremental and that their dinner together is just the beginning of reestablishing a relationship.

4. Magnification or Minimization of Mistakes

The fourth red flag of the fixed mindset is your take on mistakes. Mistakes mean that you aren't good enough. Therefore, when you inevitably slip up and make a mistake, it may be magnified in your mind and sometimes even feel catastrophic. Fixed mindset makes extreme predictions about the consequences of mistakes. Even worse—because mistakes are seen as a threatening sign that you aren't good enough—you may tend to negate, minimize, or ignore a mistake when you make one, leaving you without an analysis of why it occurred.

Check off the self-talk you have heard when you have made a mistake, and add other examples.

☐ *Disastrous!*

☐ *Catastrophic!*

☐ *Terrible!*

☐ *Horrible!*

☐ *Will never get over it!*

☐ *Will never recover!*

☐ *Will never live it down!*

☐ *Will ruin my life!*

Growth Mindset Antidote: Mistakes Are Opportunities for Growth

With a growth mindset, mistakes may not be relished, but they are to be expected. You understand that mistakes are part of getting better. They mean you are honing your skills. If you are not making any mistakes, you are not challenging yourself. In fact, you may be stagnating. In the growth mindset, mistakes are neither magnified nor minimized. Mistakes are acknowledged, studied, and investigated. You think about how to fix them. You ask yourself, *How did this happen? What can I learn from this? How do I improve? What steps may I take next time?*

Fixed mindset self-talk: A sales associate who hopes to become a sales manager mispronounces a valued client's name and says to herself, *What a stupid mistake! I will never keep this account.* Or conversely, the sales associate may completely ignore this mistake without asking herself if she has spent sufficient time reviewing the client's particulars.

Growth mindset self-talk: A sales associate who hopes to become a sales manager mispronounces a valued client's name and says to herself, *Oh no! How did this happen? I read the name on her name tag and made an assumption about how it should be pronounced. In the future, I'll double-check pronunciations of difficult names with my colleagues, or I could tell the client that it's important to me to pronounce their name correctly and ask them to kindly repeat it to me.*

In contrast to the sales associate with the fixed mindset, who viewed the mistake as catastrophic, within the growth mindset the sales associate acknowledges the mistake and then forges a plan for preventing a similar mistake in the future.

Fixed mindset self-talk: A prelaw student gets a C on an economics midterm and says to himself, *It's over, I will never get into law school!* Or, conversely, the student says, *No worries. I'll ace the rest of the exams.*

Growth mindset self-talk: A prelaw student gets a C on an economics midterm and says to himself, *Crap. Wish I would have received a better grade. This may have an impact on my GPA and my chances for law school. It is the midterm. What can I do to improve here? I'll meet with the teaching assistant to figure out where I messed up. Maybe also need to consider that study group that I passed on last week.*

Note that the prelaw student with a growth mindset doesn't feel ecstatic about the mistake. However, unlike the prelaw student with the fixed mindset, he neither catastrophizes (*I'll never get into law school*) nor dismisses or avoids the mistake (*No worries. I'll ace the next test*). Within the growth mindset, the prelaw student is accepting of challenges and a poor performance, he makes a realistic assessment of its potential impact on his future, and then forges a plan for improving his performance.

5. Viewing Others as Judges When You Are Praised or Criticized

The fifth red flag of a fixed mindset is how you interpret praise and criticism from others. When you fall into a fixed mindset, you are concerned with looking like you have enough. In the presence of someone you consider important, you ask yourself whether they think of you as adequate or not. Thumbs up or thumbs down? There are no shades of gray in your perception of their judgments, and your feelings about yourself are dependent on their opinion of you.

You may also assume that people are judging you and jump to a conclusion or try to read their minds about what they think of you. This pattern is often indicated by self-talk that takes the form of *They think I'm x,* where x is an all-or-nothing evaluation of your worth. Check off any of these thoughts you have had when praised or criticized, and add other examples.

☐ *He thinks I'm the best/the worst.*

☐ *She thinks I'm smart/stupid.*

☐ *He thinks I'm a loser/a winner.*

☐ *She thinks I'm special/a nobody.*

☐ *He thinks I'm beautiful/unattractive.*

☐ _____

Growth Mindset Antidote: Viewing Others as Resources

Rather than assume others are judging you, you see people whose opinion you value as possible sources of information for development. Your self-talk centers around gathering information for increasing your skills. Therefore, the questions that you ask yourself are *What may I learn from them?* and *How may they help me in acquiring more skills? How do I elicit helpful and specific feedback from them about improvement?*

Fixed mindset self-talk: A salesperson reviewing recent sales trends in a presentation receives feedback from his supervisor that he has missed an important data point. He says to himself, *She must think I'm an idiot.*

Growth mindset self-talk: A salesperson reviewing recent sales trends in a presentation receives feedback from his supervisor that he has missed an important data point. He says to himself, *That is an important data point. It really changes my analysis of the trends. How did I miss this? What can I do next time to be more thorough in my analysis? Let me include this point in my analysis and then discuss it with my supervisor.*

Whereas the salesperson in a fixed mindset is caught up in thoughts about what his supervisor thinks of him, the person in a growth mindset sees an opportunity for improvement. Again, unless the supervisor calls him an idiot out loud, he really does not know what his supervisor thinks. She may or may not be making that judgment. Within a growth mindset, however, what the supervisor is or is not thinking about the salesperson is less relevant to him than gathering specific information for improvement. In a growth mindset the salesperson is using the feedback from his supervisor to render a plan for increasing his sales presentation skills.

Fixed mindset self-talk: At a company cocktail party surrounded by younger associates who are listening to his opinion about the auto industry, a Wall Street trader thinks, *These guys think I'm a superstar.*

Growth mindset self-talk: At a company cocktail party surrounded by younger associates who are listening to his opinion about the auto industry, a Wall Street trader thinks, *They appear to be interested in this topic. I'll ask them about their perspective on the auto industry.*

Note that in contrast to the Wall Street trader with a fixed mindset who mind-reads that his associates are judging him, albeit positively, as a superstar, in the growth mindset positive global judgments are less important than gathering specific information for improvement. In a growth mindset, the Wall Street trader seizes the opportunity to connect and to learn from others, even younger associates. In a fixed mindset, the trader may feel good, thinking that others view him as a superstar, but he misses a potential opportunity for genuine connection with his associates and a chance to gain a perspective that may increase his trading skills.

It is very possible that others are making judgments about you, perhaps positive, perhaps negative. Again, however, unless they say it to you directly, you may never know what their thoughts are, because you cannot read their minds. Whatever their judgments may be, in a growth mindset you use positive and negative interactions with others as an opportunity to learn. Thus, even if the other person is a harsh critic, there may be something to glean if you can understand the specifics of their criticism and evaluate it in terms of your goal for improvement. Additionally, even if someone praises you profusely, when you take on a growth mindset, that praise may not be valuable unless it gives you specific information supporting change or improvement.

6. Competitive Comparisons with Peers When Hearing of Their Successes or Failures

The sixth red flag for a fixed mindset is your outlook on others' triumphs and defeats. Fixed mindset makes competitive comparisons, and news about the victory or defeat of others speaks to your adequacy. It is a virtual contest that determines if you measure up: you are superior if they flounder and inferior if they prevail. When you find yourself thinking about others' attainments, listen for the following competitive comparisons. Remember the comparison may be positive or negative. Check off any of these thoughts you've had while hearing about others' successes or failures, and add other examples.

☐ *I'm better/worse than her.*

☐ *I'm more/less attractive than him.*

☐ *I'm tougher/weaker than her.*

☐ *I'm smarter/dumber than them.*

☐ _____

Growth Mindset Antidote: Constructive Comparisons with Peers

Whereas fixed mindset uses others as yardsticks to measure yourself against, growth mindset examines how others have improved. This constructive comparison drafts a blueprint of what practices may be helpful for continued expansion.

You look to others for clues as to how they attained their proficiency. When someone is better than you, your thoughts take the form of *They appear to be skilled at this. How did that happen? What did they do? How much did they practice? What worked for them? What resources did they seek to help them? What may I learn from their experience?* When you compare yourself to those who are less skilled than you, you also have an opportunity to learn from them. That is, what did they do or not do? How much effort did they exert?

Fixed mindset self-talk: A young woman begins her new job at a high-tech company. After her orientation with other entering employees, she thinks, *I'm the smartest person in the room.*

Growth mindset self-talk: A young woman begins her new job at a high-tech company. After her orientation with other entering employees, she thinks, *There are a number of people here with different experiences and educational backgrounds. How can I use this opportunity to work with them and to further my skills?*

Rather than making a competitive comparison and assuming that she is the smartest person, the young woman with a growth mindset seizes the opportunity to make a constructive comparison and learn from her colleagues. She is focused on learning from others.

Fixed mindset self-talk: A single woman, upon learning of a former classmate's recent engagement on Facebook, says to herself, *Easy for her to find a husband. She's perfect.*

Growth mindset self-talk: A single woman, upon learning of a former classmate's recent engagement on Facebook, says to herself, *This reminds me that I would also like to be in a relationship. I know that a relationship was also important to Jan, and I'd like to talk to her about how she met her partner. I know that she spent a bit of time on dating websites and attended many social events on her own. She was also open about letting friends know that she was interested in meeting someone.*

The woman with a growth mindset acknowledges that her former classmate has something that she would like: a relationship. However, rather than conclude that her classmate is perfect, she asks what her classmate has done to find a relationship. This approach seeks information to bring about what she wants to have, whereas the competitive comparison of the fixed mindset yields nothing for finding a relationship.

In summary, inevitable situations like making a mistake or receiving praise may jar you into a fixed mindset. Without awareness, fixed mindset reroutes you to a place where you feel safe but are off course. For example, you receive criticism and give up on something you care about, because you don't want to look foolish. You can spot when that happens by training yourself to listen for fixed mindset self-talk. Your job is to recognize automatic fixed mindset thinking patterns and wire in growth self-talk.

Let's return to the pitching analogy of trying to improve your curve ball. The coach has said to shorten your stride: to change your curve ball, you need to recognize the old habit—a long stride—and then wire in a new habit, a shorter stride. Through practice, you mindfully identify the old curve ball pattern and rehearse the new pattern, so you can execute it under pressure, like the last inning of the big game when there are no outs and the bases are loaded. The next two exercise drills will help you access growth mindset self-talk when you need it.

Practice Identifying Fixed Mindset Thoughts

The following are snapshots of people from all walks of life who exhibit fixed mindset thoughts. In the space provided after each snapshot, identify what types of fixed mindset thoughts are being expressed. Use these abbreviations for the six types:

A/N = All-or-none judgments about self when faced with a challenging task

-E = Negative view of effort when a task is a struggle

100/0 percent = Perfectionist standards when assessing performance

Mag/Min = Magnification or minimization of your mistakes

VJudge = Viewing others as judges when receiving feedback

-CC = Competitive comparison

Example: A pharmacist is called in by her manager, who shares a complaint from a customer about a delay in the refill of her prescription. The pharmacist thinks, *They think I'm a goof-off. I'll never get a raise now!* Answer: VJudge, Mag/Min

Note that a good strategy for tackling this exercise is to ask, what is the potential growth-limiting situation that they encountered? In the example, the pharmacist received feedback from a person in authority, her manager. The pharmacist's response shows that she sees the manager as a judge: *They think I'm a goof-off.* Her thinking pattern is to view authorities as judges. It also appears that she sees herself as having made a mistake, and her thinking pattern reflects a magnification of that mistake with the thought *I'll never get a raise.*

1. On morning rounds, a medical intern jumps in with a response to the chief resident's question about a case, after a fellow intern stumbles. Upon reciting the correct answer, he thinks, *I'm the best there is in this program, and everyone knows it!*

   _____

2. A young man has been in email contact with three women through an online dating service. One of the women declines to meet him in person at a coffee shop. He thinks, *I'm such a loser. Jason was able to find a relationship online after only two weeks.*

   _____

3. A veteran of Afghanistan has a friend who suggests that she seek help for some problems with sleeping and nightmares. The vet says to herself, *She must think I'm a wack job. I'm strong enough to handle this on my own—don't need a shrink analyzing me!*

   _____

4. A violist receives word that she has not made the cut for a community orchestra. She says to herself, *What a horrific audition I gave! All that rehearsing for nothing! I don't have what it takes to make it professionally as a musician.*

   _____

5. During a teacher's conference, a mother receives feedback that her seven-year-old seems to be struggling with some of his math assignments. The mother thinks, *How dare she criticize Jack. Can't she see that I've done everything to help him succeed?*

   _____

6. After a second interview at a tech start-up, a recent college graduate receives word that he is no longer being considered for the job. He tells himself, *I'm not creative enough for these tech start-ups. I'm just wasting my time.*

   _____

7. A woman at an office party engages in a lengthy and enjoyable conversation with a colleague. Toward the end of the evening, he excuses himself and shifts his attention to someone else. The woman thinks, *What's wrong with me? Clearly I'm not as interesting to him as she is. This professional networking is just not worth it.*

   _____

8. A high school senior receives word that she has been accepted by two top colleges. She is the only senior to receive two such acceptances. She thinks, *Always knew I would best my classmates! I rock!*

   _____

9. After a two-year engagement, a woman's fiancé calls it off, telling her that he's not ready for a commitment after all and would like to date others. She thinks, *What an idiot I've been. I've wasted two years when I could have been dating other people. He never really thought I was good enough for him.*

   _____

10. A bank manager is called in for her yearly performance evaluation by the bank vice president. The evaluation is essentially a positive checkoff for almost all of the items. She says to herself, *Finally been recognized for my true talents. It will be smooth sailing to the top from now on!*

_____

11. After months of preparation for the MCATs, a college junior receives a disappointing overall score. He thinks, *I'm such a bad test taker. This means I'll never get into my top-choice medical schools. Alice didn't even study, and she has great scores. This will ruin my life.*

_____

12. After thirty-one years with a major insurance company, a man with two children in college is laid off from what he had considered his dream job. He thinks, *I'm a failure. How can I face my family now? I've been irresponsible. Haven't socked away enough savings.*

_____

Answers:

1. A/N, -CC, VJudge

2. A/N, -CC, 100/0 percent

3. VJudge, A/N

4. A/N, VJudge, 100/0 percent, -E

5. VJudge, 100/0 percent

6. A/N, VJudge, 100/0 percent, -E

7. A/N, -E, VJudge

8. A/N, -CC, VJudge

9. VJudge, -E, A/N.

10. A/N, VJudge

11. A/N, -CC, Mag/Min

12. VJudge, 100/0 percent, A/N

If you breezed through this exercise, great! If you found it difficult, know that it often takes a bit of practice to identify these thinking patterns.

Practice in Identifying Growth Mindset Thoughts

Now take the same situations from the previous exercise, but this time notice how the people involved exhibit growth mindset thoughts. After each snapshot, jot down the growth-thinking patterns that best match their thoughts. Use these abbreviations for the six types:

ASkills = Analysis of your current skills when faced with a challenging task

+E = Positive view of effort when a task is a struggle

Any percent = Any percent is something when assessing performance

AMistakes = Analysis of mistakes

VResource = Viewing others as resources

+CC = Constructive comparison

Example: A pharmacist is called in by her manager, who shares a complaint from a customer about a delay in the refill of her prescription. The pharmacist thinks, *This is a legitimate concern. What happened? How late was the prescription? What suggestions does the manager have about improving my efficiency?* Answer: AMistakes, VResource

1. On morning rounds, a medical intern jumps in with a response to the chief resident's question about a case, after a fellow intern stumbles. Upon reciting the correct answer, he thinks, *That seems correct, but I wonder if the other interns have another perspective on this case?*

   _____

2. A young man has been in email contact with three women through an online dating service. One of the women declines to meet him in person at a coffee shop. He thinks, *We've only been emailing for a week, and not every woman I reach out to will be comfortable meeting me in person right away. She seems interesting, so maybe I'll email again and ask if we can just talk on the phone. Jason was able to find a relationship online after only two weeks, so I could ask him how he thinks he was able to establish a relationship so quickly.*

   _____

3. A veteran of Afghanistan has a friend who suggests that she seek help for some problems with sleeping and nightmares. The vet says to herself, *My friend is trying to be helpful. I think of myself as a strong person, and yet she can see that I am struggling a bit. I wonder if she has some specific suggestions for finding resources to help me with my sleep problems.*

    _____

4. A violist receives word that she has not made the cut for a community orchestra. She says to herself, *I am disappointed. I so wanted to be a part of that orchestra! Maybe it's unrealistic to expect to be called back for everything I try out for. Parts of my performance were good. I didn't stumble on any of the notes, but I could work on my tempo and perhaps take a risk with a piece that's more challenging. Maybe I could ask the orchestra director if he has some suggestions about improving my auditions. It won't hurt to ask! I would eventually like to play with a group of professional musicians, and I may need to look at more informal opportunities to practice with others before I do that.*

    _____

5. During a teacher's conference, a mother receives feedback that her seven-year-old seems to be struggling to complete some of his math assignments. The mother thinks, *I'm surprised. I thought Jack was doing well! I wonder if she has observed any patterns? What is she seeing as his strengths and weaknesses in his assignments? What strategies does she suggest for tackling his weaknesses? Are there some specific ways in which I could be helpful to him?*

    _____

6. After a second interview at a tech start-up, a recent college graduate receives word that he is no longer being considered for the job. He tells himself, *Too bad. This seemed like a wonderful opportunity. I thought I did well at communicating my strengths and how I could contribute to the company, yet I did struggle with the exercises given to all applicants, where we were asked to solve puzzles requiring us to think outside the box. I want to gain practice in doing these types of puzzles. Will research this online.*

    _____

7. A woman at an office party engages in a lengthy and enjoyable conversation with a colleague. Toward the end of the evening, he excuses himself and shifts his attention to someone else. The woman thinks, *I really enjoyed speaking with him. Before I leave, I'll ask if he would like to share his contact information. Any new acquaintance I make is a step in the right direction. That's what professional networking is all about.*

    _____

8. A high school senior receives word that she has been accepted by two top colleges. She is the only senior to receive two such acceptances. She thinks, *I am so excited. I appreciate that not everyone gets into these schools. I spent time researching my top choices, honing my personal essays, and engaging in extracurriculars, while putting in effort in my coursework.*

_____

9. After a two-year engagement, a woman's fiancé calls it off, telling her that he's not ready for a commitment after all and would like to date others. She thinks, *So hurt and sad! Clearly this is his choice, and yet I would like to understand why he changed his mind. Is there something I could have done differently, or is this more about him? Is there anything to be learned from these two years with him?*

_____

10. A bank manager is called in for her yearly performance evaluation by the bank vice president. The evaluation is essentially a positive checkoff for almost all the items. She says to herself, *How fabulous to get such a review! I have put in a lot of effort and have made it a point to stretch myself in this job by taking on extra responsibilities. It is really important for me to progress in my career. What other skills might be needed to progress in this environment? I could follow up with the VP concerning her input about this.*

_____

11. After months of preparation for the MCATs, a college junior receives a disappointing overall score. He thinks, *So upsetting! I didn't get the score that I'd hoped for. I stumbled in some parts and did well in others. But overall it is a score that gives me a chance at some medical schools on my list. I have an opportunity to retake the test. I'll ask Alice what she did to prepare.*

_____

12. After thirty-one years with a major insurance company, a man with two children in college is laid off from what he had considered his dream job. He thinks, *Losing this job sucks. It will take some time to find a new one. Why was I laid off? Was there something in my performance reviews, or maybe it has to do with the decline in profit of the company? I'll find out. I've put away some savings, and yet as a family we will need to pull together and budget. I'm sure my family will be upset, and yet challenges like this can make us even stronger.*

_____

Answers:

1. +CC, ASkills, VResource

2. +CC, Any percent, ASkills

3. ASkills, VResource

4. ASkills, Any percent, VResource, +E

5. VResource, Any percent

6. ASkills, VResource, Any percent, +E

7. ASkills, +E, VResource

8. A/Skills, +CC, +E

9. ASkills, VResource, +E

10. ASkills, +E, VResource

11. A/Skills, +CC, A/Mistakes, VResource

12. ASkills, VResource, Any percent

You also can practice spotting fixed- and growth-mindset thought patterns by observing how others respond to life's challenges (fixed mindset potholes). These can be real people in your daily life, characters in movies, personalities in the media, and even people depicted in songs.

Ask yourself, do they seem to be responding effectively to these challenges? Try keeping a log of your observations for a week either in your journal or by downloading a weekly observation log at http://www.newharbinger.com/48299. Include the following information in your log: Whom did you observe? What pothole did they encounter? What were their thoughts or reactions? What were their fixed- or growth-mindset thinking patterns?

How to Talk Back to the Fixed Mindset with Growth Self-Talk

Fixed mindset stands ready to misdirect you when conditions open the door for it. It gets you to focus on your adequacy and sacrifice your aspirations. You now can spot the self-talk that signals its presence. How do you resist its powerful pull? The answer is to stand firm by talking back to it with growth mindset thinking. In this section, you will learn two specific techniques to defy fixed mindset thoughts and shift to growth mindset thoughts: growth mindset charting and growth mindset coaching.

The first technique, growth mindset charting, tackles the three components of a fixed mindset: thoughts, emotions, and behaviors. In this chapter we will focus on self-talk (thoughts). You will learn how to use the growth mindset chart to tackle fixed mindset emotions in chapter 4 and fixed mindset behavior in chapter 5.

Technique 1: The Growth Mindset Chart

I generally have a growth mindset, but at times when writing this book I faced obstacles that threw up clods of fixed mindset thoughts, emotions, and responses. One instance was when I grappled with the design of the computer template for the growth mindset chart! The chart would be an important tool to help readers tackle the fixed mindset and build a growth mindset platform. It was a technically challenging task for me. I felt frustrated and annoyed as I bumped up against hitches and complications with formatting. Can you see the telltale trigger for a fixed mindset in this process?

Eventually I was able to see my foiled attempts at designing this chart not as a hindrance but as an opportunity: my fixed mindset while creating this chart could be used as an example of how the chart shifts you from a fixed to a growth mindset.

In summary, what you see in this example is the final result of a very long, arduous, and exasperating process. During it, I used growth mindset charting techniques to make my way out of a fixed mindset to a growth mindset. I was pleased that the charting worked for me! But be a skeptic, and see if this technique works for you.

Growth Mindset Chart Example

Describe your fixed mindset pothole: *Trying to design and lay out this chart.*

Circle the type of pothole: (1) facing your challenging task; (2) experience of effort; (3) evaluating progress; (4) making a mistake; (5) praise or criticism; (6) the success or failure of others

FM Thoughts	FM Pattern	GM Pattern	Shift Questions	GM Thoughts
I'm computer illiterate! I can't even make a header. Can't keep the entire table on one page without the rows jumping to the second page! This should not take so long. Others don't struggle like this. I'll never figure this out.	(All-or-none self-judgment)	Analysis of current skill	What is my analysis for improvement? How do I move forward to what I value?	So, I have taught myself to do a number of things on the computer. I'll look at the help section for more info on how to proceed.
	(-Effort)	+Effort	What is a realistic view of the amount of effort required?	I have not tried to make this type of table insert before, so it will take some effort.
	100 percent/ 0 percent performance	Any percent as something	On a continuum, where am I now with progress? What is realistic improvement?	It has taken more than an hour, but I am pretty much there except for the headers. I will master this shortly.
	(Mistakes as catastrophes)	Mistakes as opportunities	What may I learn from my mistake? What can I do differently?	Okay, so I learned how not to move the column. I will continue to experiment.
	Others as judges	Others as resources	Are they offering me useful, actionable information?	My daughter knows how to format charts and tables, as does my bookkeeper. Will ask them.
	(Competitive comparison)	Constructive comparison	What may I learn from others? Is there something to be learned from their success?	

Using the Growth Mindset Chart

You can use the growth mindset chart whenever you encounter a fixed mindset pothole and notice signs of fixed mindset self-talk, emotions, and behaviors. Note that a shift in your emotions as you move toward some valued goal can be a red flag indicating that the chart may prove useful to you.

Here are a few tips for using the chart. Start by describing your fixed mindset pothole and the type or types of situation it represents. Then in the first column, write down your fixed mindset thoughts. Try to be very specific. Ask yourself what exactly was going through your mind. Write these thoughts down verbatim. Next identify your fixed mindset (FM) thinking patterns by looking at each of your thoughts separately. Ask yourself which pattern of FM thinking best captures the thought. After you spot a FM thinking pattern, circle it in the second column. Do this for each thought.

Looking at my thoughts, I could see that *I am computer illiterate* is labeling myself in black-and-white terms as a computer illiterate, which is an example of all-or-none self-judgment. I realized that the thought *I can't even make a header. Can't keep the entire table on one page without the rows jumping to the second page!* is captured under 100 percent/0 percent assessment of performance. And the thought *This should not take so long* is an example of underestimating and undervaluing effort. The thought that *Others don't struggle like this* is a competitive comparison. Finally, *I'll never figure this out* reflects the pattern of seeing mistakes as catastrophes, in that an error is magnified and viewed as catastrophic. That is, this mistake becomes an indication that I will never be able to complete the chart.

The ability to step back and categorize your FM thoughts is important, because it allows you to gain some distance from these FM thoughts and begin to make the shift to alternative growth-mindset (GM) thoughts. Once you've identified your FM thinking patterns, you can begin to consider alternatives.

Shifting to the growth mindset can be difficult, especially when you come across a pothole that seems enormous. For example, you may confront some very difficult challenges, like getting negative or positive feedback from someone whom you respect or admire more than almost anyone in the world or making a mistake that has had major consequences. To assist you with this type of shift, the chart includes GM thinking patterns in the third column. Being able to see an alternative GM thinking pattern when you are mired in FM thinking will facilitate your escape from both small and large obstructions. Looking at my FM and GM patterns in the chart, for example, I could see that an analysis of my current skill level would shift me away from the all-or-none self-judgment of *I'm computer illiterate*. Additionally, viewing mistakes as opportunities would shift me away from seeing my mistakes as catastrophes, and so forth.

To further support your shift from FM thinking toward GM thinking, the fourth column lists some questions to ask yourself. These questions will tug you out of the FM thinking rut to help you formulate GM thoughts. In my own chart, for example, the shift question *What is a realistic view of the amount of effort required?* allowed me to step back and consider that this is the first time I've tried to make this type of table and that tackling something new usually requires some effort. Similarly, the question *What may I learn from others?* shifted me out of the competitive comparison of *Others don't struggle like this* and into a constructive inquiry in which I realized that both my daughter and bookkeeper would be good resources.

As you begin to generate growth mindset thoughts, write them down in the fifth column on the chart. Returning to the example of constructive comparison, once I realized that my bookkeeper and my daughter might have information about helping me with computer tables, I saw that I didn't have to do this on my own. This was not a competition. I could look to others as resources. I then wrote down my growth mindset thoughts in the fifth column: *My daughter knows how to format charts and tables, as does my bookkeeper. Will ask them.*

It is important to write down your growth mindset thoughts. The act of writing out these responses reinforces them and makes them more readily available. That is, through writing down growth mindset responses, you are training your brain to more automatically connect with growth mindset. This type of practice is especially important preparation for life's deep sinkholes. It is a bit like a basketball player practicing her free-throw skills before the play-off game or like a concert pianist rehearsing their piece again and again before a performance at Carnegie Hall. The more you train, the more likely you can connect to skills under pressure. We are trying to help you make this growth mindset shift when the stakes are high. Shifting your mindset takes this type of preparation. Think of the growth mindset chart as regular exercise for rewiring your brain. As you gain practice in using it, the frequency, intensity, and duration of your fixed mindset thoughts will decrease and the frequency, intensity, and duration of growth mindset thoughts will increase.

As you go through your week and move forward in your growth goals, notice when your emotions shift. You may feel, for example, irritated, uncomfortable, or frustrated in pursuit of your next steps. You may notice some fixed mindset self-talk or that you are procrastinating. Use this as an occasion to try out the growth mindset chart.

Growth Mindset Chart

Describe your fixed mindset pothole: _____

Circle the type of pothole: (1) facing your challenging task; (2) experience of effort; (3) evaluating progress; (4) making a mistake; (5) praise or criticism; (6) the success or failure of others

FM Thoughts	FM Pattern	GM Pattern	Shift Questions	GM Thoughts
	All-or-none self-judgment	Analysis of current skill	What is my analysis for improvement? How do I move forward to what I value?	
	-Effort	+Effort	What is a realistic view of the amount of effort required?	
	100 percent/ 0 percent performance	Any percent as something	On a continuum, where am I now with progress? What is realistic improvement?	
	Mistakes as catastrophes	Mistakes as opportunities	What may I learn from my mistake? What can I do differently?	
	Others as judges	Others as resources	Are they offering me useful, actionable information?	
	Competitive comparison	Constructive comparison	What may I learn from others? Is there something to be learned from their success?	

You can download copies of the growth mindset chart for thoughts, emotions, and behaviors at http://www.newharbinger.com/48299. You will have opportunities to master growth mindset charting for emotions and behaviors in chapters 4 and 5. Now let's turn to another technique to assist you in shifting your self-talk from a fixed to a growth mindset.

Technique 2: Growth Coach Worksheet

With a fixed mindset, the goal is to ascertain whether you are adequate. Both adoring and harsh critics can provide the spark for self-judgment and ignite a fixed mindset. Both exaltation and denunciation can fan the flames of aggressive self-comparisons with others, minimize the importance of effort, and heighten your focus on measuring how good you are. It can deflect you from your growth goal.

So how do you recast adoration and harsh criticism into clear and specific directions for how to improve? You can use the growth coach worksheet. This worksheet will help you be a compassionate yet strategic coach when you hear passionate praise or severe criticism (whether coming from others or yourself). This is the coach who understands these natural reactions when your performance outstrips or falls short of the mark, and yet gets you back on the path toward your growth goal. This is the coach who attends to your development, does an analysis, and forges an explicit plan to build on the positives and to brave the negatives.

Here's an example of how to use the worksheet in response to harsh, critical self-talk. A single, working mother forgets that she has a scheduled parent-teacher conference for her eight-year-old, Miguel. She had hoped to get some insight into some of her son's difficulty with math. But her heart sinks and she feels angry at herself when she realizes that she missed her appointment, launching into a volley of severely critical self-talk. She used this growth coach worksheet to regain perspective:

Harsh Critic/Adoring Fan Self-Talk	Compassionate Yet Strategic Coach
What an idiot I am! If I had an ounce of brains, I wouldn't have missed this teacher–parent conference. So embarrassing. This shouldn't have happened. I'm not organized enough. Miguel's teacher will think I'm a bad mother.	It's upsetting that I missed the teacher–parent conference. How did that happen? I have a lot going on with my job and didn't check my personal calendar this morning. Maybe I could get into the habit of checking the calendar with my morning coffee. This doesn't mean I'm a bad mother. I really care about Miguel's progress. I will reach out to his teacher, apologize, and see if I can reschedule in person or by phone.

Notice in the left column of her growth coach worksheet, she wrote down her harsh, critical thoughts. Then in the right column, she responded like an understanding yet helpful coach, acknowledging her strengths and weaknesses with a specific plan to tackle weaknesses.

How would such a harsh critical voice impact your own motivation, if this were you? Do you see how the strategic coach acknowledges mistakes and then focuses on learning from them and moving forward toward what you value?

The next example shows how Kassandra used the worksheet in response to adoring fan self-talk. Kassandra loves tennis and has been playing since the age of seven when she attended a summer tennis camp. She is captain of her high school team, which faces off the first-ranked team early in the season. Kassandra narrowly beats her opponent, Jess, in a heated singles match. Her teammates and fans gather around her, singing her praises. Here is her growth coach worksheet:

Harsh Critic/Adoring Fan Self-Talk	Compassionate Yet Strategic Coach
I rock! Such a superstar! Jess didn't have a chance. I showed her who rules! Nothing can stop me now. I dominate.	So excited to win, and I played extremely well, and it helped that I've been practicing every day, every chance I get. It was a close match. How did I pull it off? I've been working on my serve and varying it. I think that helped. What did I learn from playing Jess? Where did I tend to miss the shot? She has a mean backhand—I struggled to return it. Need to focus more on that, find someone with an awesome backhand and practice returns.

Note the difference in the adoring fan self-talk and the strategic coach responses. Kassandra is clearly and understandably thrilled about her victory. Yet, how might labeling herself a superstar get in her way? Will it help her practice or continue to improve? How might she feel if she held tight to the view that she is a superstar and then lost a match? How do her strategic coach responses spur her forward? What impact might such responses have on her motivation to continue to train and hone her skills?

Now it's your turn to try out the growth coach worksheet. Reflect on your own experiences. Do you recall a time in the past when you were striving to develop and you encountered a harsh critic or adoring fan as you proceeded? Do you recall who was doing the talking? Was it your voice or someone else's voice that got in the way? What were you doing and what did you hear them saying?

Alternatively, have you encountered a harsh critic or adoring fan as you've moved toward your growth goal that you outlined in chapter 2? If you can't recall a particular time when a harsh critic or adoring fans have gotten in the way, no worries. Instead, just imagine judging your performance as you approach a goal, seeing yourself in all-or-none terms, provoking comparisons with others, playing down the significance of your effort, and maximizing or minimizing your innate ability or attribute. When you slip up, you are a harsh critic; when you do well, you are an adoring fan. Which of these ways would you be likely to judge yourself?

Now ask yourself what a compassionate yet strategic coach would say in response to your self-judgments? How would they challenge you with growth mindset questions? What questions would this coach ask? How would they assist you in creating a path toward improvement? What concrete steps would they suggest?

Use the growth coach worksheet to see what you can do to challenge and reframe your harsh critic and adoring fan responses.

Growth Coach Worksheet

Instructions: Respond to the harsh critic or adoring fan with the advice of a compassionate yet strategic coach. Write down your self-talk on the left, and on the right respond as an understanding, helpful coach would, acknowledging your strengths and weaknesses with a specific plan to improve.

Harsh Critic/Adoring Fan Self-Talk	Compassionate Yet Strategic Coach

You can use the growth coach worksheet whenever the voice of a harsh critic or adoring fan gets in the way of improvement. You can download copies of the worksheet at http://www.newharbinger. com/48299.

In this chapter you have learned some specific ways to tackle fixed mindset self-talk, or thoughts. As you shift from fixed mindset thoughts to growth mindset thoughts, you may notice a corresponding change in your emotions. That is, when you can shift to growth mindset thoughts, you may find that you feel less angry, anxious, or upset. But sometimes your fixed mindset emotions may be so powerful that you need to deal with these emotions more directly. For example, you may feel incredibly disappointed or angry at yourself for making a big mistake at your job or feel especially exceptional and unassailable when you beat out a colleague for a promotion. When this happens, it helps to have some additional ways to bump down the intensity of those feelings. Furthermore, it's helpful to learn methods to tolerate such feelings without acting on them. In the next chapter, you will learn how to address fixed mindset emotions so that you become more open to growth mindset emotions.

Summary

The fixed mindset may be automatically triggered by the following situations (or fixed mindset potholes):

- Facing your valued, challenging task

- Experiencing the task as effortful and difficult

- Evaluating your progress.

- Making mistakes

- Criticism or praise from others, especially authorities

- Hearing about the success or failures of peers

When you are flooded by fixed mindset thoughts, you can respond with growth mindset thoughts to get back on track:

- Analysis of current skill or attribute when faced with a challenging task (in response to all-or-none judgment of self)

- Viewing effort positively when a task is difficult (in response to viewing effort negatively)

- Any percent-is-something standard when assessing progress/performance (in response to 100 percent-or-nothing standard when assessing progress or performance).

- Viewing mistakes as expected and as opportunities for growth (in response to magnification or minimization of mistakes)

- Viewing others, especially authorities, as resources (in response to viewing others as judges or mind reading)

- Constructive comparisons with peers when hearing about their successes or failures (in response to competitive comparison with peers)

The growth mindset chart and growth coach worksheet are two techniques that will help you talk back to the fixed mindset with growth mindset challenges.

CHAPTER 4

How to Deal with Fixed Mindset Emotions

In this chapter you will learn to spot fixed mindset emotions and develop ways to deal with them so that they don't block your opportunities for exploration and change. Even when you have been driving forward with a growth mindset, one of the six potholes, like a mistake or criticism, may jolt you into a fixed mindset. With a fixed mindset, feelings like embarrassment can throw you off track, hold you back, and prevent you from pursuing what's important to you. However, if you stay in touch with mood shifts when you face these types of stumbling blocks to growth, you will have a window into your mindset. If you can spot fixed mindset emotions, you can take steps to decrease their power and open yourself up to the growth mindset.

A shift in your mood may be your first sign of a fixed mindset. That is, you may notice a change in your feelings before you notice any particular fixed mindset thoughts. Of course, everyone's emotions naturally rise and fall during the course of the day. Some of these fluctuations may be minor, like irritation at a driver who does not signal a left turn, or they may be major, like dread at having to undergo chemotherapy. Variations in your feelings are part of being human. Yet a swing in your emotions is a clue about your mindset when the emotional swing follows a fixed mindset pothole.

The Emotional Clues

A fixed mindset is not just about negative emotions, nor is a growth mindset only about positive emotions. With a fixed mindset, you feel good when you look proficient at something and bad when you look deficient. Thus, you experience glee when you are given an assignment that looks difficult to others but is simple for you. With a growth mindset, growth is your goal, so you feel good when growth is possible and bad when it isn't. With a growth mindset, you might feel bored when assigned a task that looks difficult to others but is easy for you.

It's natural for a fixed mindset to evoke an emotional response, such as anxiety about looking bad or smugness about looking good. It's important to remember that there's nothing wrong with these emotions, in and of themselves, but you do want to be careful that they don't cause you to avoid opportunities for growth. The first step in letting go of these constraining emotions is to label them. See them as an important signal. Learn from them. Use them as an opportunity to practice your growth mindset strategies. Try not to judge yourself for having them, such as *Here I go again with the same reaction. This means I can't change.* Start with giving yourself credit for simply recognizing a fixed mindset emotion. The intensity, duration, and frequency of these emotions will diminish as you learn to develop a growth mindset.

If fixed mindset emotions can hamper your progress, how may growth mindset emotions foster it? What exactly is a growth mindset emotion? A growth mindset emotion is about a mindful openness to your world. It is a state of ready calmness. It is about a connection or involvement in a non-judgmental way with the different aspects of the self, others, and the world that may be relevant for development. On a continuum of feeling, it ranges from negative (dullness or flatness when you are not growing) to neutral (calm, acceptance, appreciation, or curiosity as you assess how to grow) to positive (flow, excitement, and enthusiasm as you grow).

Below are the six potholes, or growth menaces, each paired with exercises to help you grasp the emotions of each mindset. These exercises will give you some practice in identifying fixed mindset sensations so that you can let them go and make room for the growth mindset.

1. Emotions When Facing a Challenging Task

An optimally challenging undertaking holds the most promise for expanding your skills; however, it is also a gamble in that it may disclose your abilities. With the fixed mindset, your concerns revolve around whether you have enough ability rather than on possibilities for growth. Will you be exposed as lacking? For example, with a fixed mindset, the safer bet for an amateur basketball player is to face off against either an easy opponent or an opponent like LeBron James whom they could not possibly beat. In either case, they avoid the difficult emotions of losing a contested match. However, with a growth mindset, the amateur pick would be an opponent with competencies that marginally exceed them. By picking an opponent for a match they could win or lose, the amateur player would risk the difficult emotions of failure.

A challenging task is either an opportunity or a threat, depending on your mindset. What are you likely to feel in each mindset? Let's explore these possible emotional responses with the following exercise.

Growth Vs. Fixed Mindset Emotions

Put yourself in the following scenes. Imagine approaching these situations from a fixed mindset. Then imagine approaching the same situations from a growth mindset. Write down your likely feelings in each mindset.

As a sales rep for a pharmaceutical company, you are asked to market medications to a large medical practice that has an account with another company. Other sales reps have tried but failed to get their business.

What would your fixed mindset emotions be?

_____

_____

What would your growth mindset emotions be?

_____

_____

As an accountant, you begin work on taxes for an important client account that appears complicated but that is easy and familiar for you.

What would your fixed mindset emotions be?

_____

_____

What would your growth mindset emotions be?

_____

_____

Some people have mainly fixed mindset emotions, some have mainly growth mindset emotions, and others tend to have a mix of emotions. The takeaway is to be in touch with what you feel when you face a demanding task. That means pausing and identifying your emotions before you begin. Sometimes these emotions are intense, sometimes small. These emotions give you a window into your mindset. Identification of fixed mindset emotions is the first step toward acceptance and letting them go.

2. Emotions in Response to Effort

How do you feel when a task is a struggle? With a growth mindset, effort is an expected part of extending your skills. When something is easy, it means you are stagnating. In a fixed mindset, exertion means you do not have what it takes and are flawed. An easy activity is a relief because it means you have lots of ability.

Growth Vs. Fixed Mindset Emotions

Suppose you are writing a mystery novel. You breeze through the construction of the plot and are spot-on with the creation of the main character. Now you are wrestling with the development of the supporting character. You sit at your computer and nothing comes easily. You spend days fabricating and then discarding ideas. It has been over two weeks, and yet a full portrait of this character remains unclear. What would you feel if you were experiencing this? Picture yourself at the end of two weeks with no coherent idea about this character.

What would your fixed mindset emotions be?

_____

_____

What would your growth mindset emotions be?

_____

_____

3. Emotions When Assessing Your Progress or Performance

How do you feel when your performance falls short? How about when your outcomes exceed expectations? An honest assessment of your progress allows you to forge a plan for future development. In a growth mindset, your development is seen on a continuum, and any improvement is seen as progress. Lack of improvement is important information and an opportunity for problem solving.

Self-assessments can also cue a fixed mindset. In this case, anything less than perfection can leave you uncertain as to whether you are adequate or whether you have what it takes to succeed.

Let's study the range of emotional reactions to self-assessments.

Growth Vs. Fixed Mindset Emotions

Put yourself in the following scene, and approach the situation from a fixed mindset. Then imagine approaching the same situation from a growth mindset. Write down likely feelings in each mindset.

You accept a job offer and move to a new city. You don't have any friends and are feeling lonely, so you develop a plan to get to know more people. You invite people in your office to lunch and ask a few neighbors out on the weekend for coffee. Additionally, you chat regularly with some new acquaintances at a gym that you've joined. You decide to host a casual dinner at your house and five out of the eleven invited guests attend.

What would your fixed mindset emotions be?

_____

_____

What would your growth mindset emotions be?

_____

_____

4. Emotions When You Make a Mistake

What are your feelings when you make a mistake? Most people experience a mixture of feelings. On your road to developing your skills, mistakes are anticipated and likely. If you made no mistakes, you would not be learning anything new or expanding your skills. On the other hand, realizing that you made a mistake can generate a fixed mindset: if you have enough ability, you don't make mistakes. Mistakes expose you as inadequate.

Growth Vs. Fixed Mindset Emotions

Imagine you are a middle school student, and your parents have been encouraging you to speak up in class. In your English class, you take a risk, raise your hand during a discussion, and voice your viewpoint about a short story. After class, your teacher calls you aside and corrects your grammar.

Imagine yourself standing there, hearing the English teacher's words. What would you feel?

Can you feel the fixed mindset emotions? What are they?

_____

_____

Can you feel any growth mindset emotions? What would they be?

_____

_____

5. Emotions When You Are Praised or Criticized

As you move toward what you value, sometimes people applaud you and sometimes they pan you. With a growth perspective, criticism or praise, if detailed and well argued, is information that you can use to improve or develop. In a fixed mindset, such feedback is a global judgment about you. When commended, you assume that others see you as remarkable, and when criticized, you conclude others see you as lacking.

Growth Vs. Fixed Mindset Emotions

You have been a nurse for seventeen years at a small hospital in the suburbs. The hospital has hired a recently graduated nurse practitioner as supervisor of your floor. On her first day, she observes you and suggests that you revise your notes on an incoming patient. You have been writing notes on patients for seventeen years. Imagine how you would react. What would you say? What would you feel?

What fixed mindset emotions might you have?

_____

_____

What growth mindset emotions might you have?

_____

_____

6. Emotions When You Hear of the Success or Failure of a Peer

How do you feel when you learn of another's remarkable achievement or when you learn of their stunning failure? With the growth mindset, this is valuable knowledge. You ask yourself, how did this happen? You understand that successes and failures are part of everyone's experience in the journey to progress. At the same time, you do an analysis so that you can advance your competencies.

With the fixed mindset, the performance of others becomes a measure of your ability or attributes. Their success means that you by comparison are not measuring up; their failure indicates that you have more ability and therefore are superior.

Growth Vs. Fixed Mindset Emotions

Suppose that you are an aspiring actress in New York City. For the last few years, you have worked in a large department store as you take voice and dance lessons. You audition for small chorus-line parts whenever you get a chance. You and a friend try out for a new off-Broadway musical. Both of you are called back for a second audition. Imagine getting the news the next day that your friend has secured a part in the chorus line but you have not. Can you imagine what you would say to your friend or how you would feel?

Can you feel the fixed mindset emotions? What are they?

_____

_____

Can you feel any growth mindset emotions? What are they?

_____

_____

How do these emotions help? How do these emotions hurt?

_____

_____

The takeaway for this section is try to stay in touch with what you feel when you face these types of stumbling blocks to growth. If you pause and name your emotions, you will have a window into your mindset. If you can spot fixed mindset emotions, you can take steps to decrease their power and open yourself up to the growth mindset.

How to Let Go of Fixed Mindset Emotions and Make Room for Growth

In this section, you will learn some techniques for letting go of forceful emotions that may keep you in a fixed mindset. These techniques are derived from evidence-based strategies for managing difficult emotions. *Managing* is the key word here. These techniques help to lessen the intensity of difficult emotions; they don't eliminate the emotions outright. Think of it as turning down the volume on a distracting false alarm so that you may continue to focus on what is vital. You can still hear the alarm ringing in the background; you accept that it is there, but you move forward with your growth steps.

For example, let's consider a student who is given a take-home exam in algebra. He easily solves the first problem. When a solution is not readily apparent for the second problem, he skips it. As he struggles with the third problem, he feels a wave of anxiety. He cannot focus; the fear is paralyzing. With his sensations of panic, it's hard to tackle thoughts like *I don't have what it takes to finish this* and move forward with thoughts like *difficulty is expected*. Using the following techniques, however, the student still notices anxiety, but it plays at a softer level in the background, allowing him to finish the test.

Almost everyone experiences intense emotions from fixed mindset thoughts, especially when you start moving toward significant goals, so these methods take some work. Your job will be to try them out, practice them, and see which method feels best to you.

Diaphragmatic Breathing

The fixed mindset threat of being revealed as deficient may trigger the sympathetic nervous system (the flee, fight, or freeze response). You breathe shallowly from your chest and narrowly focus on the threat; such breathing changes your chemistry and prepares your body for action to cope with a looming menace. With a fixed mindset, however, the threat is not a physical menace but a psychological one—the threat of being exposed as inadequate—so shallow breathing and other physiological changes aren't helpful.

With deep breathing, you can tap into the parasympathetic nervous system (the rest-and-digest response), allowing you to reset and be open to the growth mindset. Deep breathing is the type of breathing that happens when you are relaxed. Such breathing originates in your diaphragm. Think of sleeping puppies or cartoon characters with their bellies slowly moving up and down with each breath. The research supports deep breathing as an effective calming strategy, and it is used by athletes, entertainers, and public speakers. You can use deep breathing to manage fixed mindset emotional reactions and open yourself up to the growth mindset.

Diaphragmatic Breathing for Fixed Mindset Emotions

Find a comfortable position. The first few times you do this, you may wish to lie flat, face up on your bed, or on the floor. Some people find it helpful to place a pillow under their knees. You may also practice this from a comfortable chair. Just lean back, release any tension from your shoulders, uncross your legs, and place both hands on your abdomen.

Note the difference between chest breathing and abdomen breathing by placing one hand on your chest and one on your abdomen.

1. Place both hands on your abdomen.

2. Inhale gently through your nose for a count of two or three (or however long feels comfortable). Notice the air traveling through your nostrils.

3. Exhale through your mouth with your lips slightly pursed for a similar count.

4. Simply let go of your breath. Note how your hands lowers slightly as you exhale

5. Practice this deep breathing for five to ten minutes. Note the rise and fall your hands on your abdomen.

Note there is no magic number of seconds (or counts) for inhaling and exhaling. Start with what feels comfortable for you. For some people, that may be two counts; for others it may be three or four. Another tip: do not force your exhale, but simply release your breath much like a balloon releases air.

Deep breathing is a skill. It takes practice. Try to use this technique a couple of times a day.

With practice, deep breathing is a portable skill that you can use anytime during the course of the day to quell fixed mindset emotions that get in the way of your growth goals.

Often I work with clients who understand intellectually that deep breathing is important but do not practice it consistently. When faced with a fixed mindset situation that elicits deep feelings, they will tell themselves to breathe deeply and are dismayed when it doesn't work. It would be like a pitcher commanding themself to throw a curve ball during a play-off game after only practicing a curve ball a few times during the season. To be effective, deep breathing needs to be performed as a ritual a couple of times daily: in the morning before you get out of bed and at night after you go to bed. With such a routine, you are prepared when fixed mindset feelings are sparked spontaneously.

Progressive Relaxation

Under a perceived threat, the muscles in your body prepare to spring into action. Think of a rabbit, very still but with muscles taut and ready to leap away from a coyote. Now let's change the scene. Suppose you are undergoing a simple dental cleaning. You may notice that your hands and fingers clench or that your legs and ankles stiffen. Even though there is no real physical risk (if your hygienist is a properly trained professional), your body experiences it as a hazard and responds accordingly.

Likewise, your body may respond to a fixed mindset challenge as it would to physical danger. For example, a graduate student going through a day of job interviews feels nervous and experiences a tightness in his shoulders and neck, even though the concern is about being exposed as incompetent. It is difficult for the student to let go of feelings of anxiety if his body is stressed. If you can learn to relax your muscles when you contend with these emotions, then you will feel them less intensely. Once relaxed, you can tackle the steps needed to fulfill your objectives.

Progressive relaxation is about systematically contracting and loosening each muscle group in your body. It teaches you to note the difference between rigid and relaxed muscles by intentionally tensing and then resting each of the major muscle groups in your body, for example, your arms, legs, neck, and head.

Although initial sessions require a bit of time, with repeated practice, you can learn to quickly note and release the tension in the major muscle groups in your body. A number of internet resources are also available to assist you with this technique. Like deep breathing, the process sounds simple, yet it takes repetition to achieve mastery. When fixed mindset emotions are formidable, simply instructing yourself to relax your muscles will not result in the desired effects unless you have practiced.

Diaphragmatic breathing and progressive relaxation are two techniques to alleviate feelings like anxiety and anger. The following two methods can also be used for such emotions, but may be particularly helpful for feelings of superiority, smugness, or contempt. These are the type of emotions that occur when you are in a fixed mindset and believe that you have what it takes or believe that you have more ability than others. Remember, these emotions can get in the way of growth.

Here-and-Now Focusing

When your goal is to grow, you focus on the world about you and seek out information that will give you material for improvement. Fixed mindset sentiments distract you from exploring that information. So, for example, the graduate student with a sense of urgency to prove his competence during an interview recites a long and exhaustive list of his accomplishments without listening carefully to the questions that the interviewer is posing. The weight of his need to prove himself crowds out the opportunity to forge a connection with the interviewer that would allow him to glean information about the job and the department.

The emotional pressure of a need to show your talents can also arise in social settings. Consider the woman sharing a coffee with a man she has met on an online dating site who spends the entire time recounting her many interests and achievements. She misses the chance to express curiosity about pursuits that he cherishes or viewpoints that he holds. She loses opportunity to discover if they share an outlook or perspective that merits another meeting.

A strategy that dampens the urgency of these fixed mindset sensations is mindfulness. One type of mindfulness that has been shown to be useful is grounding yourself in the present moment. Sometimes called here-and-now focusing, it is about taking time to monitor each of your senses and asking yourself *What am I perceiving at this instant?* The exercise immerses you in the world about you by helping you to tune into these impressions. The advantage of such a process is that it opens you up to the present, making room for the described growth mindset sentiments.

Try this out informally with the following exercise. .

Focusing on the Here and Now

Begin by turning to your breath. Simply notice your breath as you inhale and exhale. Feel the sensation in your nostrils as air enters and leaves your nostrils. Notice your breath without trying to change it.

After a few moments, turn your attention to your sense of sight, sound, and touch. If your mind wanders, gently bring your attention back to what you are perceiving with these senses in the here and now.

What sounds do you hear? Notice distinct noises in the foreground. Note what you hear more distantly in the background. Hear soft sounds, louder sounds. Tune in to those sounds: if your mind strays, gently bring it back to the sounds in your surroundings. For example, if you hear a car engine in the background and think about your own car, notice that thought without judging it, and bring your attention back to the here-and-now sounds around you.

Now what do you see? Notice the colors, shapes, shadows, and textures in your immediate surroundings. Note colors, see their redness or greenness. See them without making a judgment. If the colors cause you to think of something else, like your child's red bike, bring your focus back to the present moment and colors. Now do the same with shapes, shadows, and textures.

What about the sense of touch? Can you feel the texture of the chair on which you sit? What about the pressure of the floor against your feet? Again if your mind wanders, so you begin to think about lunch, that's okay. Bring your attention back to the immediate touch sensations. The roughness or smoothness of the arm of your chair. Let thoughts outside these immediate sensations float out, and return to the present sense.

This informal exercise is an introduction to mindfulness techniques. There are many more to be found on audio, in books, and on apps. You can learn on your own or go to classes. Give the technique that appeals to you a chance, and try it out a couple of times a day for fifteen to twenty minutes for a couple of weeks.

Cultivating mindfulness takes practice. Doing so through these techniques can help you resist those urgent fixed mindset sensations and allow you to sustain your openness to the world around you, making space for growth.

FLOAT

I have developed a method called FLOAT that will help you get some distance from intense fixed mindset emotions. The acronym serves as a prompt to notice, identify, and tolerate fixed mindset emotions and take growth steps in the face of them. It has roots in mindful meditation, distress tolerance, and A.T. Beck's AWARE (Beck, Emery, and Greenberg 2005) and is designed for fixed mindset emotions that get in the way of your growth goals.

F—Feel changes in your emotions when you encounter a growth mindset menace

L—Label the specific emotion

O—Observe the emotion as a natural consequence of a fixed mindset

A—Accept the emotion without judgment; such emotions are expected

T—Take your growth mindset step despite the emotion

Maria's story illustrates the use of this FLOAT method for dealing with strong emotions.

Maria is a sales representative in an appliance store where she aspires to become manager. During the annual appliances sale, a customer curtly asks her where the sale freezers are, and then, as Maria tries to point out the available models, bolts past her demanding assistance from "someone who knows what they are doing." Maria feels frustrated and irritated; she can barely conceal her feelings and has an urge to abruptly turn her back on the customer and retreat to her desk. What is the growth menace that Maria has encountered? Can you see that these emotions are related to that challenge? How can she deal with these emotions so that she can effectively respond to this difficult customer?

Here's how Maria used the FLOAT method:

F—Feel the change in your emotions. Maria notes the shift in her emotions as she deals with this criticism.

L—Label the specific emotion. She labels her emotion as frustration and irritation.

O—Observe the emotion. She views the frustration and irritation as a natural consequence of a fixed mindset.

A—Accept the emotion without judgment. She tells herself that such emotions are expected.

T—Take the growth mindset step despite the emotion. In spite of these feelings, she makes a growth mindset choice in keeping with her aim to be a store manager. Store managers learn to deal with difficult customers. She empathetically acknowledges the customer's need for more information and assures him that he can either talk to her or speak to a senior associate.

Very much related to FLOAT are mindful meditation exercises for emotions. Mindful meditation is about watching or observing your emotions with acceptance and acknowledgment, without feeling a need to engage with your emotions. This type of mindfulness practice is analogous to seeing a gray cloud in the sky roll by you. You observe the cloud, are aware of it, and watch it pass. You do not engage with the cloud or try to halt it, nor do you run from it. You are aware of it without feeling a need to judge it or respond to it. Again, this takes some practice but can be helpful in assisting you in making the fixed mindset emotion less intense.

In summary, you now have four methods to subdue fixed mindset emotions when they are especially intense. These include diaphragmatic breathing, progressive muscle relaxation, here-and-now focusing, and the FLOAT method. The aim of these techniques is not to eliminate fixed mindset emotions but to decrease the intensity, frequency, and duration of unhelpful emotions and to create space for the growth mindset. At the heart of these strategies is appreciating that as a human being you will experience fixed mindset emotions that may become dominant when you pursue a very valued growth goal and encounter a pothole. When these expected emotions occur, try to notice them, be aware of them, and accept them without judging them. Experiment with some of the above techniques. Try to have a growth perspective about acquiring these methods. Try to build them into your daily routine.

Using the Growth Mindset Chart to Make Emotional Space for Growth

Now that you have had some practice in identifying and letting go of fixed mindset feelings, let's incorporate these techniques into the growth mindset chart that you started in chapter 3. This time we'll focus on your feelings rather than your thoughts.

Growth Mindset Chart

Describe your fixed mindset pothole: _____

Circle the type of pothole: (1) facing your challenging task; (2) experience of effort; (3) evaluating progress; (4) making a mistake; (5) praise or criticism; (6) the success or failure of others

Filling out the chart: Write down your fixed mindset (FM) thoughts in the first column, and circle the FM patterns in the second column that capture these thoughts. Then shift to a growth mindset (GM) pattern by asking yourself the shift questions. In the fifth column, write down your GM thoughts in response.

Write down your FM emotions and circle their intensity: mild, moderate, or intense. Then respond to the shift questions and write down your GM emotions.

FM Thoughts	FM Pattern	GM Pattern	Shift Questions	GM Thoughts
	All-or-none self-judgment	Analysis of current skill	What is my analysis for improvement? How do I move forward to what I value?	
	-Effort	+Effort	What is a realistic view of the amount of effort required?	
	100 percent/ 0 percent performance	Any percent as something	On a continuum, where am I now with progress? What is realistic improvement?	
	Mistakes as catastrophes	Mistakes as opportunities	What may I learn from my mistake? What can I do differently?	
	Others as judges	Others as resources	Are they offering me useful, actionable information?	
	Competitive comparison	Constructive comparison	What may I learn from others? Is there something to be learned from their success?	

FM Emotions	FM Pattern	GM Pattern	Shift Questions	GM Emotions
(mild/moderate/intense)			How may I tolerate this? How do I calm myself?	

Start by writing down your fixed mindset emotions in the first column, and circling their intensity, whether mild, moderate, or extreme. Ask yourself the shift questions, and write down some strategies that you'll use: diaphragmatic breathing, progressive relaxation, mindfulness techniques, FLOAT, or any others. Then, in the last column, write down your GM emotions after practicing one of the above strategies.

Some people find it easy to identify their specific fixed mindset emotion. For example, you may be able to quickly name *envy* as your emotion when hearing a friend has beaten you out for a part during an audition. Alternatively, you may find it difficult to identify a specific emotion and may simply experience a general feeling of unease upon hearing of your friend's recognition. That's okay. The idea is to notice the shift in your emotion and do your best to record it in the chart. It is acceptable to simply write "upset" or "uneasy" or "uncomfortable." After writing down your emotion, rate how intense the emotion is by circling mild, moderate, or extreme.

Next review the shift questions: *How do I tolerate this? How do I calm myself?* There may be several ways to do this. Write down strategies, like diaphragmatic breathing, progressive relaxation, mindfulness, or others that have been helpful to you. When you have powerful fixed mindset emotions, it is difficult to move toward growth.

Now practice one of these strategies until you can lessen the impact of these emotions. Engage in this calming strategy until you can accept or tolerate the feelings. Sometimes that may mean a brief break from the situation, returning to it at a later time.

Let's return to my growth mindset chart to illustrate how to do this:

Growth Mindset Chart Example

Describe your fixed mindset pothole: *Trying to design and lay out this chart.*

Circle the type of pothole: (1) facing your challenging task; (2) experience of effort; (3) evaluating progress; (4) making a mistake; (5) praise or criticism; (6) the success or failure of others

FM Thoughts	FM Pattern	GM Pattern	Shift Questions	GM Thoughts
I'm computer illiterate! I can't even make a header. Can't keep the entire table on one page without the rows jumping to the second page! This should not take so long. Others don't struggle like this. I'll never figure this out.	(All-or-none self-judgment)	Analysis of current skill	What is my analysis for improvement? How do I move forward to what I value?	*So I have taught myself to do a number of things on the computer. I'll look at the help section for more info on how to proceed.*
	-Effort	+Effort	What is a realistic view of the amount of effort required?	*I have not tried to make this type of table insert before, so it will take some effort.*
	100 percent/0 percent performance	Any percent as something	On a continuum, where am I now with progress? What is realistic improvement?	*It has taken more than an hour, but I am pretty much there except for the headers. I will master this shortly.*
	(Mistakes as catastrophes)	Mistakes as opportunities	What may I learn from my mistake? What can I do differently?	*Okay, so I learned how not to move the column. I will continue to experiment.*
	Others as judges	Others as resources	Are they offering me useful, actionable information?	*My daughter knows how to format charts and tables, as does my bookkeeper. Will ask them.*
	(Competitive comparison)	Constructive comparison	What may I learn from others? Is there something to be learned from their success?	

FM Emotions	FM Pattern	GM Pattern	Shift Questions	GM Emotions
(mild (moderate) intense)			How may I tolerate this? How do I calm myself?	
Frustration, irritation			*Deep breathing. FLOAT.*	*Acceptance, appreciation*

Underneath the section on fixed mindset thoughts, I fill in my fixed mindset emotions. When struggling with designing this chart, I had thoughts like *This shouldn't take so long* and *I'm computer illiterate.* So under FM emotions in the first column, I write down *frustration* and *irritation,* and circle *moderate* for both. After I ask the shift questions, I decide to do some deep breathing and use the FLOAT method. My emotions settle, and I feel appreciation and acceptance and write those sensations under GM emotions.

As mentioned earlier, a shift in your feelings can sometimes be the first clue that you've fallen into a fixed mindset pothole. In this case, it can be helpful to grab a copy of the growth mindset chart and write down your FM emotions before doing anything else. Return to the top of the growth mindset chart and review the six potholes. Ask yourself, *Prior to the shift in my emotions, did I encounter one or more of the growth potholes?* If the answer is yes, then your emotions indicate that you have fallen into a fixed mindset. Do you recall or remember any self-talk that accompanied these emotions? If so, then capture these thoughts in the growth mindset chart as described in chapter 3.

Summary

- Powerful fixed mindset emotions leave little room for growth.

- Your emotional reactions may be your first clue to your fixed mindset.

- Tune into changes in your emotions, and ask yourself if your feelings are associated with one of the six fixed mindset potholes.

- Note whether these emotions reflect a focus on judging your adequacy versus a focus on growing your skill.

- Practice your calming strategies regularly so that under pressure you can dampen fixed mindset emotions and open yourself up to growth mindset feelings.

Use the growth mindset chart to identify your fixed mindset emotions and bring down the intensity of your feelings when you hit a pothole.

CHAPTER 5

A Growth Mindset Action Plan to Resist Fixed Mindset

The road to your goals is pitted with discouraging situations that may jolt you into a fixed mindset. Without your awareness, fixed mindset takes control and guides your actions. Obliviously, you steer toward destinations that feel familiar and safe but hold little possibility for exploration or expanding your world. You swerve and accelerate away from places that offer the possibility of growth, because they expose you as wanting. You spin toward a road that looks treacherous but is well known to you, so you look like a champion. Or conversely, you choose a path that is extremely difficult, because when you don't succeed you still look heroic.

If you can scout out the behavioral detours that signal a fixed mindset, you can use them as signposts to get back on the growth mindset road. Below, you'll learn to spot the fixed mindset by watching for the telltale reactions to potholes. You'll learn to pivot from these and map out a growth mindset action plan to get back on track. On the growth road you seek and embrace information useful for improvement with the appreciation that the quest will reveal imperfections and limitations.

How to Identify Reactions That Signal a Fixed Mindset

Here are six telltale fixed mindset reactions to potholes.

1. Reactions to Your Challenging Task

You make many choices about what to do during the course of your day. If you're doing something that is of little importance to you, you're likely to slide into the easiest method. You find a simple routine to tidy up your house in the morning before work. This saves time for things that are more significant like breakfast with your children or walking your dog. However, when you want to make changes, your usual choices may not be optimal for growth.

To make an important change in your life, such as increasing your cardio fitness to deal with heart disease, you need to shake up your comfortable routine. Such a change requires mindful choices in keeping with your self-improvement goal. Growth mindset says to check out the new cardio health class offered at the local Y even if it may be a bit challenging. But fixed mindset can get in the way: it warns that the new fitness class will show how weak and unfit you really are, so you stay with your usual morning stretch routine. Growth mindset deliberately chooses activities that stretch you even when they are a bit discomforting. Fixed mindset pulls you back to the routine that is customary and safe, as new activities may reveal deficiencies.

How do you know if your everyday choices are steered by a fixed mindset? Let's return to Alexandra, whom you met earlier. She made some progress on steps to renovate her apartment, grow her career, and meet new friends. One day she reflected on her life satisfaction questionnaire and realized that she really wanted a long-term relationship. Were her choices in keeping with this goal? She was socially active. She had two or three friends that she would regularly meet for dinner, drinks, and a movie. She had known them for a couple of years, and it was effortless to get together with them. She also was comfortable at meetings of an environmental group and felt relaxed about participating. However, was this predictable way of socializing in line with finding a long-term companion? Was she a bit too content with these familiar activities? Was the fixed mindset confining her to what feels safe?

What activities would Alexandra consider if she wished to develop a relationship? What options might take her out of her comfort zone? What first steps might she take that would help her do this?

Alexandra came up with the following ideas, which made her feel uneasy but would increase her chances of a potential relationship:

- Create and post on an online dating platform

- Reach out to a couple of people in her environmental advocacy group that she found interesting or attractive, to see if they would meet her for coffee

- Let her friends and family know that she would like to eventually be in a long-term relationship and ask if they could introduce her to someone

The above action steps were uncomfortable for Alexandra. Fixed mindset asks, *Am I attractive? Am I interesting?* Within a fixed mindset, Alexandra can avoid unwanted responses to these questions by choosing the safe and easy route, taking the painless track of hanging with the friends she knows. Growth mindset asks, *What paths move me toward what I value?* With a growth mindset, Alexander asks, *How do I get closer to finding someone I could share my life with?* She takes these new, somewhat difficult steps and accepts she will feel a bit nervous as she breaks from her customary habits.

With a fixed mindset, the easy and familiar option often seems the most appealing even though it is not beneficial in terms of your growth goal. Now let's look at another side of the fixed mindset and how it drives your behavior. With a fixed mindset, the extremely risky option may seem especially appealing. Remember Jessica, who had difficulty coping with her divorce? In addition to disparaging her ex to her children and friends, she falls into a pattern of flirting with married or already committed men. Why might she find these unavailable men alluring? How is this behavior consistent with a fixed mindset?

After a divorce, fixed mindset asks, *Am I attractive?* And how does Jessica avoid any unwanted answers to these questions? Fixed mindset chooses the extremely difficult undertaking of getting the attention of someone who is in another long-term relationship. Such actions sidestep any unfavorable conclusions about her desirability. If unavailable men rebuff her, it's no reflection on whether she's attractive or interesting enough, because they are constrained by their commitments. She avoids the possibility of being revealed as defective. What's more, with this route, if she succeeds at getting their attention, it validates how attractive she must be. Sadly, however, she misses the opportunity to connect with available prospects, bringing her nearer to a sustainable relationship.

When you're trying to stretch yourself, you deliberately make choices that promote your growth—somewhat risky, moderately challenging activities. To illustrate, if you wish to improve your tennis game, your best choice is an opponent who is slightly more skilled than you. The game will be more evenly matched, and the game will take longer, giving you more of a chance to bump up your tennis abilities. You will win some points and lose some points, which will show your weaknesses. With a longer game, you may observe that you won most of the shots with your forehand and lost most of the shots on your backhand. Your takeaway is that you need to practice or perhaps modify your backhand. You have little opportunity to recognize a problem with your backhand and hone this skill if you play an easy opponent and beat them handily in every game. On the other hand, playing Roger Federer would not be a wise choice (unless you are Rafael Nadal), as he would beat you swiftly and you would have little opportunity to figure out how to improve your game.

When you want to make a change in your life, watch out for the telltale signs and ask if you are automatically slipping into the easy, comfortable choice, so you don't fail, or are going for the extremely risky choice, because failure is expected. If you can spot the safe and familiar preferences of a fixed mindset, then you can pivot to the path that takes you out of your comfort zone and fosters growth.

Pivot to an Opportunity for Growth

Review your life satisfaction questionnaire. Are there personal or achievement areas that you value but have not tackled? Have you slipped into a routine that feels safe and comfortable but does not afford a chance to expand or explore? Is it possible that your avoidance signals a fixed mindset? How would you know?

Write down the important area of your life that you have neglected. Have you been playing it safe or making especially chancy choices?

_____

_____

Brainstorm options to improve in this aspect of your life by answering the following questions in the space provided.

What would you elect to do if you did not care about being bad at it?

_____

_____

What activities move you away from feelings of monotony or safety but feel a smidgen scary?

_____

_____

What would you try if you were not concerned about looking silly?

_____

_____

What risks would you take if you felt you had enough ability?

_____

_____

Be aware of your choices when your intention is to grow. Ask yourself if a comfortable or an extremely difficult undertaking is undermining you. What would you consider if you wished to grow? What first steps might you take that would help you do this?

_____

_____

Purposely go for the moderately challenging venture which optimizes your chances for improvement. Put specific action steps for activities into your calendar.

2. Reactions When a Valued Undertaking Is Difficult for You

How do you behave when something you care about is really hard for you? You're committed to it, but you find it physically or mentally demanding? Your responses to effort are clues to your mindset.

Let's look at Alexandra, who decided to improve her fitness with yoga. During an intermediate yoga class, one pose is especially strenuous for her. Alexandra's responses to this pose being tough to execute are clues to her mindset. Alexandra redoubles her effort to hold the pose as she focuses carefully on her instructor's directions. She practices the pose at home several times during the week and continues class despite the increasing difficulty of more advanced poses. These reactions signal a growth mindset. Growth mindset says effort is expected when you wish to be fit. You accept that getting fit won't be easy, and you increase your persistence in the face of difficulty.

What reactions to the taxing pose would signal a fixed mindset? Fixed mindset says difficulty means you're not cut out for yoga: if you have the ability, it would be easy. How would this impact Alexandra's determination to hold the pose? Would she bother listening to the teacher's instructions? Would she put in the time to practice at home? Would she quit the class as the exercises became more arduous?

You may find that the first steps toward growth are easy for you. It's your reactions to increasing difficulty that signal your mindset. So tune into your reactions when you find yourself struggling with something important to you. Practice with the following exercise. Put yourself in another's shoes, grapple with the sensation of exertion, and predict how you would behave under each of the mindsets.

First imagine you are a college sophomore, and your dream is to become a pharmacist. Two days before your final biology exam, you attend a review session led by a teaching assistant. During the review, you struggle with understanding the functions of mitochondria. The concept is not coming readily. Envision experiencing such difficulty. Conjure up the tension as you ponder and struggle with the concept. What are your likely actions? Do you revamp your focus and ask questions to clarify the different functions, or do you start texting some friends? Do you stay for the entire review session, or do you dart out before it is over? What might you do the night before the exam? Do you leave extra time to review the concepts while studying after dinner, or do you hang with your friends most of the evening and then cram during the wee hours of the morning?

Fixed mindset asks, *Am I competent?* Difficulty means you don't have what it takes to become a pharmacist. How do you escape from this unpleasant conclusion? Avoid the activity where you struggle: text friends, leave class early, procrastinate. These actions signal the fixed mindset. On the other hand, growth mindset expects effort as you learn the skills of a pharmacist. It directs you to concentrate and persist when something is difficult; the harder you try, the smarter you get. Immersion in the material—including staying for the entire review session and putting in extra time to review difficult concepts—signals the growth mindset.

Spot the Mindsets in Your Responses to Difficulty

To detect your own responses to something difficult, close your eyes and recall taking steps toward something that you valued. Perhaps it was playing a musical instrument, learning a new sport, or developing a new relationship. What was that activity?

_____

At some point did you experience the undertaking as demanding? Picture that moment when you felt like you were struggling. What was happening? Where were you? Who was there?

_____

_____

What did it feel like to you?

_____

_____

How did you react? For example, did you feel distracted? Did you try to distance yourself mentally or physically? Did you pivot to an unrelated activity? Or did you increase your determination? Did you intensify your focus? Did you take steps to become more engaged or connected with the activity?

_____

_____

What did your reactions signal, a growth mindset or a fixed mindset? Almost everyone has had some fixed mindset reactions when they struggle with something important. It is a very common response, especially if other things have come easily for you. What is key is that you detect those fixed mindset reactions so you can deliberately shift to the growth mindset.

As you move toward change, tune into your responses to effort. Ask yourself if your actions reflect a growth mindset with increased focus, engagement, and persistence, or do they reveal a fixed mindset with distraction, escape, procrastination, and resignation?

3. Reactions to an Evaluation of Your Progress

How do you behave after you assess your headway on something you care about? Your behavior signals your mindset. Let's consider two different scenarios to illustrate this.

First, put yourself again in the shoes of the college sophomore who's just taken a difficult biology exam. In class the professor hands back your biology exam, a mix of multiple choice and short essays. You see a red C- written at the top. You also see that the professor has written extensive comments.

Stop and consider how you might respond. Do you look at the grade and quickly put the exam in your backpack, telling friends in the class that you just did not feel well during the test? Do you set aside time to read the professor's comments, or do you throw it into your desk when you get back to your dorm without ever looking at it again? Do you make an appointment to discuss your exam with your professor during office hours?

Fixed mindset says ability is unchangeable. It may be high or low, but there's little you can do about it. Fixed mindset says that if you are really smart, special, or superior, progress should be swift and the results perfect: you should ace the biology test. Progress evaluations are good or bad, with no shades of gray. Any appraisal less than 100 percent is unacceptable. The C- grade means your inadequacy is uncovered. Fixed mindset says you can't change your ability, so manipulate how you appear. Cover up your deficiency by making excuses for the grade—saying that you did not feel well during the test—so you don't look inept. Flee from evaluation entirely, so as to avoid any unwanted information about your insufficiency—throw the test into your desk when you get back to your dorm and never look at it again.

Growth mindset says that although you may start out with a certain amount of ability, you can improve it. The skills to be a pharmacist are built over time, so your standard is incremental. Any improvement is acceptable, even if it is slight. Progress is measured on a continuum, and small steps are seen as making headway. You are realistic about what your current skill level is, and use appraisals of progress as clues for how to take a step forward. The C- is disappointing, but growth mindset steers you to accept it and do an analysis. Attempts to gather information for ways to improve signal a growth mindset—you take the time to read the professor's comments and make an appointment to discuss the exam during office hours.

As another example, imagine you are Marcel attending your fifteenth high school reunion. After graduating, you moved away from your hometown and started a landscaping business. This is the first time you've gone to a reunion, and you hope to reconnect with past friends and make new ones. In a conversation, a former classmate tells you about his work—he has opened an auto repair shop. As he talks, you realize that starting your own business has not been smooth sailing—you have had some ups and downs in hiring employees and gaining clients.

Now consider how you would react to this interaction, depending on your mindset.

Would you monopolize the conversation, exaggerate your financial success. and magnify the extent of your client base? Would you interrupt your classmate when he's speaking and direct few questions his way? Would you tune out and turn away without sharing anything about your own business? Or, alternatively, would you relate both the triumphs and trials of starting your new company, soliciting his input about the challenges of getting competent help and marketing his business?

Your mindset can be detected in your reactions to self-appraisals; you realize that starting your own business has not been easy. Fixed mindset says progress should be smooth sailing, a straight line to great and dedicated employees and lots of clients for your business. Anything short of that indicates you have failed—you're incompetent. With this painful answer to your self-appraisal, your choices are to hide your failure to yourself and others—tune out and turn away from your former classmate. Alternatively, you can hide your inadequacy by spinning or inflating your actual accomplishments—exaggerate your financial success and magnify the extent of your client base.

Growth mindset says that although you may not have all the skills for your landscaping business, you can build them over time. Progress is measured on a continuum in small steps with the acceptance that financial success will not be immediate. You make a realistic assessment of how you're doing in the business, issues with hiring employees and increasing your customer base, and use it as the starting point for an analysis of how to grow. Reactions to this self-appraisal are to seek out information that will assist you with the growth of your new company. A conversation with your former classmate in the auto repair business is an opportunity to share your challenges in starting your new company; you get his thoughts about how to get competent help and market your business.

Spot the Mindsets in Your Reactions to an Evaluation

Reflect back on a time when you were prompted to consider your progress in an area that mattered to you. What was the situation? Was it an interpersonal or an achievement setting?

_____

_____

Do you recall the moment when you were prompted to consider your progress? What exactly was happening? Who was there?

_____

_____

How did that information affect you?

_____

How did you portray the results of that appraisal to yourself or to others? Did you make excuses to yourself or others if your performance fell short? Did you describe your performance with hyperbole, overstating your actual performance to yourself or others?

_____

_____

Did you seek out specific information for improving?

_____

Did your behavior foster or hinder chances for growth? How?

_____

_____

As you tackle undertakings that you care about, be on guard for that moment when there is an evaluation of your progress. Pause and consider your choices at that instant. Can you resist inflating your performance? Can you skip the alibi when your performance falls short? Can you authentically depict your strengths and acknowledge your weaknesses so that you can gain ways to improve?

4. Reactions to Your Mistakes

What do you do when you discover that you've made a mistake? Your reactions indicate your mindset.

Let's return to Alexandra, who has attained her certificate as a paralegal and has been awarded a promotion in her company with many new and exciting responsibilities. Her boss asks her to assemble and forward an important document to the in-house attorney for review. Mistakenly, she emails the document to an out-of-house attorney, revealing confidential information about the important client. How would you feel if you were Alexandra and you recognized your error?

How would your mindset affect your next steps? Would you report the mistake to your boss, profusely apologize, and immediately offer to resign? Would you quickly phone the out-of-house attorney and ask him to delete the document, as it was sent in error, and not mention the mistake to your boss? Would you analyze what led you to make this error, report it to your boss with your analysis, and get their input for dealing with the error?

Fixed mindset says mistakes mean you're not good enough. Mistakes shout your inadequacy to the world. With a fixed mindset, Alexandra can succumb to the devastating conclusion that she's not cut out for her new job, thereby offering her resignation to avoid further embarrassment. Or, she may hide the mistake from her boss or blame someone else for it so as not to expose her incompetence.

Growth mindset says mistakes are an expected part of getting better. If you don't make any mistakes, you're not doing anything challenging. With a growth mindset, Alexandra accepts that with her promotion and the new responsibilities, mistakes will be inevitable. Although this mistake is understandably upsetting, her reactions are to figure it out. Was she rushing to submit the document? Did she double-check the email address? Was she distracted by other priorities? She shares the mistake with her boss and develops protocols to guard against future slipups, and becomes a better paralegal.

Mistakes are tough to deal with. Some mistakes can feel devastating because of their far-reaching consequences. It's natural that your initial reactions to big mistakes be governed by the fixed mindset. Most people will find that they have mixed reactions to a mistake. What's important is that you detect fixed mindset reactions, like ignoring the mistake, hiding it, or camouflaging it, so that you can mindfully choose growth mindset behaviors like acceptance and an honest analysis with concrete steps for corrections. In the previous chapters, you learned to detect fixed mindset emotions and self-talk when you make a mistake. You can also spot fixed mindset by paying attention to your behaviors.

Spot the Mindsets in Your Reactions to a Mistake

Think back to a time when you made a mistake as you pursued something that was of significance to you. Or consider the types of mistakes that you may make as you take steps on your life satisfaction questionnaire.

Describe the mistake. What was the setting? Was it social, personal, or related to career, work, or achievement?

_____

_____

Put yourself in that moment when the mistake was revealed to you. What did you feel?

What did you think? Were you alone or with others?

_____

_____

How did others respond?

_____

_____

What were your reactions? Did you attempt to hide the mistake? Did you try to camouflage it by blaming others? If so, whom did you blame?

_____

_____

Did you dismiss the mistake as unimportant or ignore it entirely?

_____

Did you acknowledge the error to yourself? Did you disclose it to others?

_____

_____

Did you reveal it to someone who is harshly critical if their words held information for improvement?

_____

If you admitted the mistake, what were your next steps? Did you do an analysis? What was your take-away from the mistake? Did you learn from it so that it informed your future actions?

_____

_____

Did you have a mix of reactions? Identify the reactions that signal a fixed mindset. How would you have behaved in a growth mindset?

_____

_____

Your response to a miscalculation may be abrupt and without consideration. Fixed mindset equates mistakes with incompetency, so the natural, immediate reaction is to hide mistakes from others—and also from yourself. When you make a mistake, take some time out to examine your possible reactions. What are your viable choices at that instant? What choices would indicate a fixed mindset? What choices would redirect you to a growth mindset?

5. Reactions to Praise and Criticism from Authorities

You turn to certain people in your life for various reasons. When you wish to hang or kick back you may prefer individuals who tend to be generally positive, fun, and cheery. You may avoid those who complain or are overly negative. Those choices may be quite straightforward. But whom do you seek out when you are trying to develop or improve? Whom do you connect with when you want feedback critical for developing your skills or attributes?

Let's return to the graduate student from chapter 4 who was applying for a job. Pretend you are this graduate student. As part of the process, you give a talk and answer some tough questions from the audience. Subsequently, you go on to meet with a team of interviewers for a total of two days. It is exhausting, but you are still very interested in the work and liked the team. A few weeks later, you receive an email thanking you for the application but informing you that another candidate has been selected.

Imagine getting this email. Think about all the hard work you have done to prepare for this possibility—years in graduate school and weeks of planning for this interview. Experience the disappointment. Almost everyone has suffered big upsets like this. Consider what you might think and feel from the perspective of each mindset.

Now what? What are your choices? To whom do you turn to help you with this dispiriting result? You instinctively reach out to some friends and family for support. You connect with the people who care about you, even when you have failed at an undertaking. They don't understand much about your work but are there with a kind word or a hug. They encourage you to revise your CV and revamp your talk, and you do so.

What then? What choices do you make under each of the mindsets? Do you get counsel from your advisors or peers about your CV and talk? Yes or no? If yes, whom do you seek out? Do you reach out to the professor who likes you, generally lauds your efforts, and yet rarely gives you much actionable advice? Or do you track down the faculty member who gives dynamic lectures and who might give you insights for changing your talk but who tends to be somewhat harsh and demanding?

Fixed mindset says authorities are judges of your adequacy. Praise from those with expertise means you're superior, and their criticism means you're deficient. Fixed mindset says avoid unflattering feedback—seek those who show only admiration and run from those who are critical. In a fixed mindset, the graduate student will approach only those who applaud his efforts and abilities.

Growth mindset says authorities are potential resources. Seek those who dispense sound and insightful instruction for improvement. Their tone may be either tough or gentle, but what's crucial is that their recommendations be spot-on with actionable steps for honing your skills. Growth mindset doesn't avoid critics if they offer concrete suggestions. With a growth mindset, the graduate student schedules an appointment with the professor who gives amazing lectures, even though he feels a bit intimidated.

Please note: I am not suggesting that you consult with someone who degrades you, calls you names, or who is universally critical. Even useful feedback from abusive authorities is not worth the pain—there are alternatives. I am describing resources who may be a bit intimidating or exacting but can make pragmatic observations about your weaknesses as well as your strengths, with specific takeaways for change.

Spot the Mindsets in Your Reactions to Praise and Criticism

Think back to a time when you pursued something important and were shot down. Maybe it was a promotion, membership on a team, or a relationship? Everyone has had these disappointing experiences. What was your disappointment? Where were you? What was happening?

_____

_____

Did you turn to others for support? If so, who were those others? How did they support you?

_____

_____

Did you turn to authorities for guidance about how to move forward? Do you remember a point when you considered getting advice from someone else? If yes, who was that someone else?

Were they able to give you helpful suggestions?

_____

_____

Did you encounter someone who was critical and yet gave you useful guidance?

_____

_____

If you did not connect with someone else for their perspective, what happened? Were there no resources available, or did a fixed mindset get in your way?

_____

_____

After a setback, it is natural and healthy to reach out to those who unconditionally care about you. However, later when you have the option to get expert help from someone else, monitor your reactions. Do you see signs of a fixed mindset—do you seek out those who applaud you and shun those who give you tough but helpful advice? If so, pause and consider the growth mindset choice: weather the hard-to-hear criticism necessary for change.

6. Reactions When You Hear of the Success or Failure of Peers

How do you react when you hear about someone's exceptional performance in something important to you? Your responses are clues to your mindset.

Let's go back to the graduate student who is dealing with the disappointment of being rejected for the job he coveted. Again, visualize being that graduate student. You are now in the process of revising your CV and your talk, when you hear some news from a friend. A classmate has received not one but two job offers! Yet another blow. What would it be like to watch your classmate excitedly share the news with faculty in the department? How would it feel as you observed her trying to weigh out the pros and cons of two very attractive options, when you had no offers? What would you think?

Ponder your next responses from the perspective of each of the mindsets. After extending your congratulations to your classmate—what do you do? Do you pull back, no longer chatting with her in your research seminar? Do you put her down behind her back? Perhaps comment to a close friend that she received two offers because she is a woman and companies are looking for more diverse employees? Or instead do you reach out to your classmate to inquire about her experiences during the interview and to get her take on the challenges and how she tackled them? Do you ask her to give you some feedback about your CV and talk?

Fixed mindset says another's performance is a measure of your adequacy. Their success means you're not good enough; their failure means you're superior. How do you deal with another's spectacular triumph? You can distance yourself from them to avoid the unflattering comparison, or you can minimize their accomplishment so that you don't look so bad. In a fixed mindset, the graduate student stops communicating with his successful peer, or he finds a way to negate her success so he doesn't appear lacking.

Growth mindset says someone else's success is an opportunity to find out how to improve. Approach them because you have a chance to learn how they did it. With a growth mindset the graduate student reaches out to the successful peer and receives hints about handling interviews and suggestions for how to tweak his CV and talk. He also maintains a connection with his classmate that may be important for his future professional development.

Spot the Mindsets in Your Reactions to Another's Success

Think back to a time when you were toiling with something important to you, and you heard of a peer's stunning success with that same undertaking. Almost everyone has these memories: someone else finds a long-term relationship when you're not meeting anyone promising; someone else loses weight and looks remarkable while you struggle to stay with a healthy diet and exercise. Or perhaps, like me, you are working on a mission you care about—writing this book—and learn that a colleague publishes yet another book when you have published zero!

Describe the scene. What were you striving for? How did you hear the news? Who shares it with you?

_____

_____

Put yourself in that moment. What did you feel and think?

_____

What did you say about your peer's success to yourself and others? Did you play down their achievement? Did you avoid them? Treat them differently after hearing the news? Or did you approach them? Did you engage with them to understand what they did to succeed?

_____

_____

Did your reactions signal a fixed or a growth mindset? If they signaled a fixed mindset, what would have been an alternative growth mindset action?

_____

_____

Growth mindset says the exceptional performance of another is your chance to understand the many moving parts involved in getting better at something. It is an occasion to dissect the different components that play a part in someone else's significant feat. Clearly, some things contributing to that person's success may be beyond your control, yet others may be a window into what you can try to do better.

Pause and consider your reactions when you learn of someone's success in an area that is important to you. Watch out for reactions marked by avoidance or belittling. While these responses are human and understandable, they indicate that fixed mindset has taken control. What's important is that you get better at detecting these signs so that you can make a growth mindset choice and get information that could help you figure out your next steps.

How to Devise Your Growth Mindset Action Plan

Fixed mindset stands ready to steer your reactions when you are rattled by potholes like those just described. How do you stand firm? The answer is to spot your self-limiting reactions and use them as a signal to pivot to growth mindset actions. Design a growth mindset action plan marked by engagement rather than avoidance. Instead of swerving around opportunities for growth, because they hold the threat of exposing your shortcomings, engage with them even when that voice in your head is asking, are you smart enough, lovable enough, good enough?

Think of it as exploring the different points along your road to growth despite your trepidation. Despite feeling unsettled, you select optimally challenging tasks, put in more effort than is comfortable, realistically assess your performance, get feedback from others, and make constructive comparisons with peers.

How do you devise and execute your action plan, despite being mired in a fixed mindset, when that voice your head and your emotions are telling you that this road is dangerous and to veer off onto the path to safety? It has to do with *acting as if* you are in a growth mindset. You engage in growth behaviors even though you are experiencing emotions like anxiety, anger, superiority, or envy. You stick to your growth blueprint even when you are questioning your adequacy.

You can do this with the FLOAT technique from chapter 4. Remember the final step in this technique that asks you to act in a growth mindset way despite fixed mindset emotions? Research shows that changing your behavior sways your emotions and thoughts. It's a challenge to stay on the growth road when your thoughts and feelings are shouting *Turn around!* With the following techniques, you can wrestle control from the fixed mindset.

Technique 1: How to Stand Firm with Your Growth Action Plan

Start by practicing the growth mindset action plan in a domain that you value *somewhat but not highly*. For example, suppose that you highly value developing your skills as a fiction writer and only somewhat value increasing your skills as a cook who entertains friends. While you may fall into a fixed mindset when you pursue either activity, it will be easier to stand firm with your growth action plan in cooking.

Here's what your plan may look like in cooking:

1. Choose a somewhat difficult task that offers the possibility for growth but feels a bit risky in terms of revealing your ability. (For example, pick a recipe that is moderately difficult, one that you would like to learn to do but is a bit tricky to execute. Do not choose a recipe that is too easy for you—so that you look like a top chef—or a recipe that is so complicated that almost anyone would be likely to fail at it. Invite a few friends over and include someone whose cooking skills you respect.)

2. Engage more fully when the task is effortful. (When the different aspects of the recipe take more effort, push onward. Try not to hide your struggle from your friends, making it look like it is easy for you.)

3. Engage in a realistic assessment of your performance. (How would you rate your execution of the recipe on a scale of 0 to 100? Try not to make excuses if it falls short or to positively exaggerate the outcome if it is good. What would you do differently? How was your timing? How would you improve the recipe? What was positive? How did you achieve that?)

4. Engage in an analysis of mistakes to further your growth. (If the sauce was too thin, ask what happened? Did you not reduce it long enough? Did you not add enough flour?)

5. Engage with those individuals who can give critical feedback helpful for growth. (Ask the guest whose cooking skills you respect most to give you some specific suggestions about the recipe and your execution of it. What did they think you did well? What would they do differently?)

6. Engage in a constructive comparison with others. (Ask your friends about cooks whom they really admire. Do they know someone who is especially good at entertaining? What specific skills have they developed that allows them to excel? For example, do they excel at baking? Roasting? Did they go to classes? Did they read certain cookbooks? Did they have a mentor?)

The more significant the area of growth, the more you need to practice in areas that are somewhat important to you. So before tackling fiction writing, the person above may choose another somewhat less important goal for growth, like learning to improve their dance moves at a club. After practicing with a growth mindset action plan for cooking and dancing, they would develop an action plan for fiction writing.

Now it's your turn to practice your growth mindset action plan. Think of an area that you somewhat value and develop a growth mindset plan consisting of the six action steps just described. It could be in a personal, social, or achievement area; it could be something you already do but haven't taken to the next level. For example, you value making things, and in your spare time, you do carpentry. You've become pretty good at creating some small decorative boxes. Consider a step up to the level where you stretch yourself, and it feels just a smidgeon uncomfortable. What is a step up from these small decorative boxes that you produce easily? Maybe it would be a complicated box or a small table? The step needs to be moderately difficult but not something extremely difficult like an entire dinette set.

Growth Mindset Action Plan

1. Choose a somewhat difficult task that offers the possibility for growth but feels a bit risky in terms of revealing your ability. (Do not choose something that is easy for you, so that you look like a star, or choose something so difficult that almost anyone would be likely to fail at it.)

   Write it down. _____

2. Engage more fully when the task is effortful. (When the different aspects of the task feel effortful, push onward. Embrace the struggle and possibly share your difficulty with a friend. Don't try to make the task look easy.)

   _____

3. Engage in a realistic assessment of your performance. How would you rate your execution of this task on a scale of 0 to 100? Try not to make excuses if it falls short or to positively exaggerate the outcome if it is good.

   _____

   What would you do differently? How would you improve it? What was positive? How did you achieve that?

   _____

4. Engage in an analysis of mistakes to further growth. What mistakes did you make? Ask yourself what happened? Can you take actions to correct it or prevent it next time?

   _____

   _____

5. Engage with others who can give critical feedback that's helpful for growth. Ask those whom you respect to give you some specific suggestions about your execution. What did they think that you did well? What do they suggest that you do differently?

   _____

   _____

6. Engage in a constructive comparison with others. Do they know someone who is especially good at your undertaking? What specific skills have they developed that help them to excel? Did they go to classes? Do they have books or websites to recommend? Did they have a mentor?

   _____

   _____

To organize other growth actions plans, you can download this worksheet from http://www. newharbinger.com/48299. As you use this worksheet, be sure to tackle each of the six action steps to develop your skills. You are acting as if you have a growth mindset as you explore these steps, even when you notice fixed mindset red flags. Continue to practice weekly using the growth mindset action plan in fields that you somewhat value. With practice, you will be ready to proceed to an area that is especially significant to you.

It's important to involve yourself in the six growth action steps despite apprehension and urges to avoid. If you start with a task that is somewhat important to you, then you gain practice and become more comfortable in exploring each of the waypoints: choosing moderately difficult tasks, putting in more effort, realistically analyzing your progress, examining your mistakes, and gaining information from others for clues for improvement.

Technique 2. Tackle a Difficult Growth Action Step with a Hierarchy

As you follow your growth mindset plan, you may discover that some of the six steps are more difficult than others. For example, some people have little problem connecting with peers to get helpful feedback but may find it tough to contact experts to gain critical information for improvement. Others may find it easy to redouble their efforts when under pressure but find it difficult to accept and analyze their mistakes so they can improve.

Do you veer away from some of the action steps? Look at your responses in your growth mindset action plan. Which of the six are you most likely to skip or avoid?

Perhaps you dodge the action step of getting feedback from others who may offer valuable guidance for improvement. Fixed mindset says these folks are judges of your adequacy so it's natural to want to avoid them. To illustrate, let's suppose you play classical violin at a music conservatory. You pretty much have a growth mindset and engage in most of the growth actions. That is, you choose moderately difficult musical pieces, you fully employ your efforts to increase your skills (practicing several hours daily), you realistically assess your progress in that you understand your strengths and weaknesses (and can see that you are indeed making some progress), you acknowledge your mistakes during a piece and analyze what happened, and you look to peers who are skilled and engage in a constructive comparison. However, where you swerve behaviorally is in asking authorities for critical feedback. When there is an opportunity to receive input from an expert at the conservatory, you avoid it. You feel anxious and, despite telling yourself that this will be an opportunity for growth, you procrastinate. You stick with the instructor who praises your performance but is not able to offer you much more insight in how to strengthen your skills, or perhaps you completely avoid getting feedback from anyone with expertise.

How about you? Do you find it relatively easy to ask experts for feedback that may be helpful for your growth, or do you at times avoid authorities who may offer important guidance? Use the hierarchy technique if this is a growth action step that you dodge. Here is how the violinist used this technique.

Hierarchy: Get Advice from Experts

Instructions: Use this worksheet if at times you avoid asking knowledgeable authorities for feedback.

1. In the first column, make a list of authorities who may be helpful, ranking them in order from easiest to most difficult to approach.

2. Begin with the expert who is least intimidating (row 1) and schedule the date when you will contact them.

3. Set up a time to meet.

4. Summarize your takeaway from the meeting. Write out specific suggestions for improvement.

Repeat the above with expert number 2, then number 3, and so on.

Rank Order	Date to Contact	Date to Meet	Takeaway from Meeting
1. Abe	3 pm today by email	Next Tuesday at 6 pm	Work on timing and lower chords
2. Abigail			
3. Theresa			
4. Gerald			

To feel at ease with getting advice from experts, the violinist starts with an instructor, Abe, who's readily approachable. He marks down when and how he will reach out to Abe. He schedules a meeting, tolerates any apprehension, and performs for Abe. Afterward, he writes down his takeaway from Abe. He is then ready to repeat the process with the next, more intimidating instructor on his list, Abigail, and so on, until he performs for his most intimidating instructor, Gerald, and receives his feedback.

With the hierarchy you gradually expose yourself to the discomfort of asking for advice from those who might be helpful to you. You can also use this same hierarchy to gain advice from accomplished peers. This hierarchy worksheet is available for download at http://www.newharbinger.com/48299. Even if you don't hesitate to get advice from others, you can use this worksheet to identify people who might be helpful and organize a plan to connect with them.

Alternatively, perhaps you dodge the growth step of analyzing mistakes. Fixed mindset says mistakes mean you're inadequate, so it's natural to avoid this action step and make excuses instead. This is another case where using a hierarchy can help you tackle a growth step.

Let's suppose you're trying to be more organized at work. You take many of the action steps. You turn to others for hints about getting organized. You accept that this may be a struggle and commit to the increased effort needed to become organized. However, you have not owned up to the many mistakes that result from your disorganization. It can be painful to admit that you missed an important deadline and natural to fall back on defending yourself.

How do you use the hierarchy technique to tackle this growth action step to engage in an analysis of your mistakes? Here's how it works with confronting mistakes of disorganization in the workplace.

Hierarchy: Confront and Analyze Mistakes

Instructions: Use this worksheet if at times you avoid confronting and analyzing mistakes.

1. Make a list of the mistakes related to your growth goal, ranking them in order from easiest to most difficult to acknowledge.

2. Begin with the mistake that is least intimidating (row 1) and schedule the date when you will confront it.

3. At that time, do an analysis to come up with a promising step to improve.

4. Implement this step daily for two weeks.

5. Under takeaways, write down how it went. Is there anything you would change or do differently?

Then continue to the next mistake on your list. Follow the same steps until you have confronted and analyzed all of your mistakes.

Rank Order	Date to Confront	Ways to Improve	Implement	Takeaways
1. Late response to important emails	Tuesday 3–4 pm	Flag emails in order of importance, and respond to important emails within twenty-four hours.	Each time I receive email over next two weeks, flag and respond to important emails within twenty-four hours. Mark two weeks in calendar.	Helpful, but need to create folders for emails
2. Miss appointments	Wednesday 3–4 pm	Immediately record in calendar with one-day alert.	Practice recording appointments for two weeks. Mark two weeks in calendar.	Helpful, but need to review appointment in morning before work
3. Miss deadlines	Thursday 3–4 pm	Divide deadline task into doable, concrete steps, create timeline, and schedule steps on calendar.	Tackle steps on calendar for two weeks. Note end of two weeks in calendar.	Procrastination on some steps. Chunk steps down even more. Try FLOAT to tolerate discomfort when facing steps on calendar.

In this example, you start with the easiest mistake to confront, which is responding late to emails. You commit to a time to tackle it, come up with a strategy to improve (flag important emails and respond within twenty-four hours—just an acknowledgment of receipt), implement that strategy for two weeks, and write down your takeaways (helpful to flag emails, but you need folders to organize your inbox). Once you've seen 75 percent improvement in this area, you repeat the process with the next mistake that you want to confront, and so on, up the hierarchy.

Looking more closely at this example, when you move on to the most difficult mistake of missing deadlines, you must tolerate fixed mindset emotions like shame and the urge to make excuses. You commit to a time to figure out how you miss deadlines and ask yourself what you might do differently. What specific steps might you take to improve? What about dividing the deadline task into doable steps, putting those steps in a timeline, and scheduling them in your calendar? You implement this plan for two weeks and then review what happened. The takeaway: you procrastinated on some steps, so next time you'll chunk the steps down even further and do the FLOAT technique to deal with discomfort.

If you make excuses for mistakes when you hope to improve, this hierarchy worksheet is available for download at http://www.newharbinger.com/48299. Start with the easiest mistake and move up to the most difficult mistake to confront. Inch by inch, you will become more comfortable with owning up to mistakes, so you can increase your skills.

Using the Growth Mindset Chart to Shift to Growth Mindset Behaviors

Let's complete the third and final part of the growth mindset chart to help you shift from fixed mindset to growth mindset behaviors. This time, your task is to recognize fixed mindset behaviors, like avoidance, procrastination, boasting, excuse-making, and come up with a specific doable plan for change that will move you closer to your valued goal.

To illustrate, here is my own example of creating the growth mindset chart on my computer:

Growth Mindset Chart Example

Describe your fixed mindset pothole: *Trying to design and lay out this chart.*

Circle the type of pothole: (1) facing your challenging task; (2) experience of effort; (3) evaluating progress; (4) making a mistake; (5) praise or criticism; (6) the success or failure of others

FM Thoughts	FM Pattern	GM Pattern	Shift Questions	GM Thoughts
I'm computer illiterate! I can't even make a header. Can't keep the entire table on one page without the rows jumping to the second page! This should not take so long. Others don't struggle like this. I'll never figure this out.	(All-or-none self-judgment)	Analysis of current skill	What is my analysis for improvement? How do I move forward to what I value?	So I have taught myself to do a number of things on the computer. I'll look at the help section for more info on how to proceed.
	(-Effort)	+Effort	What is a realistic view of the amount of effort required?	I have not tried to make this type of table insert before, so it will take some effort.
	100 percent/ 0 percent performance	Any percent as something	On a continuum, where am I now with progress? What is realistic improvement?	It has taken more than an hour, but I am pretty much there except for the headers. I will master this shortly.
	(Mistakes as catastrophes)	Mistakes as opportunities	What may I learn from my mistake? What can I do differently?	Okay, so I learned how not to move the column. I will continue to experiment.
	Others as judges	Others as resources	Are they offering me useful, actionable information?	My daughter knows how to format charts and tables, as does my bookkeeper. Will ask them.
	(Competitive comparison)	Constructive comparison	What may I learn from others? Is there something to be learned from their success?	

FM Emotions	FM Pattern	GM Pattern	Shift Questions	GM Emotions
(mild (moderate) intense)			How may I tolerate this? How do I calm myself?	
Frustration, irritation			Deep breathing. FLOAT.	Acceptance, appreciation

FM Behavior	FM Pattern	GM Pattern	Shift Questions	GM Behavior
Drink coffee and eat ice cream instead of working. Look at grill pans in Crate and Barrel catalog.	Choose too easy or very difficult tasks	Choose optimal challenges	How do I design a doable, step-by-step growth mindset plan? When will I start?	Work on it from 8 to 9 a.m. the next day despite frustration. During that time use the help section on the computer. Set up meeting times with bookkeeper and daughter for tutorial—sharing with them about my progress and mistakes.
	Decrease/hide effort	Increase efforts	How long will I stay with my plan (despite the effort)?	
	Excuses or exaggerations of progress	Accurate assessment of progress	What are my strengths and weaknesses? How do I move forward from weaknesses?	
	Hide mistakes	Analyze mistakes	What steps do I take to move forward from this mistake?	
	Seek those who praise and avoid critics	Seek critics who give helpful information	Who can give me helpful information? When will I use these resources?	
	Devalue/avoid successful others	Analysis of another's success	What steps have others taken to be successful? Can I take those steps?	

In my example, I capture the fixed mindset behaviors marked by avoidance and procrastination. I write down in the first column under FM behavior: *Drink coffee and eat ice cream instead of working. Look at grill pans in Crate and Barrel catalog.* I circle these FM behavior patterns: choose an easy or very difficult task and decrease/hide effort.

I then ask myself, *What would my behavior be if I had a growth mindset marked by engagement? How do I engage with a specific growth plan?* I consider the shift questions and ask myself: *How do I design a doable, step-by-step growth mindset plan? When will I start the task? How long will I stay on task? How will I analyze mistakes and evaluate progress? Who or what will I use as resources to analyze mistakes and progress? When will I use these resources?*

And responding to these prompts, I then write down my growth behavioral plan in the column under GM behavior. Remember, it's important to implement your growth behavioral plan by finding a designated time to start with a specific step. In the example, I set up a time the next morning after breakfast from 8 to 9 a.m. During that time, I commit to working on the chart, despite the frustrations. I also note to set up appointments to consult with my bookkeeper and daughter.

Now it's your turn.

Growth Mindset Chart

Describe your fixed mindset pothole: _____

Circle the type of pothole: (1) facing your challenging task; (2) experience of effort; (3) evaluating progress; (4) making a mistake; (5) praise or criticism; (6) the success or failure of others

Filling out the chart: Write down your fixed mindset (FM) thoughts in the first column, and circle the FM patterns in the second column that capture these thoughts. Then shift to a growth mindset (GM) pattern by asking yourself the shift questions. In the fifth column, write down your GM thoughts in response.

Write down your FM emotions and circle their intensity: mild, moderate, or intense. Then respond to the shift questions and write down your GM emotions.

Write down your FM behaviors, circle the FM behavior patterns, respond to the shift questions, and write down your growth behavioral plan under GM behavior.

FM Thoughts	FM Pattern	GM Pattern	Shift Questions	GM Thoughts
	All-or-none self-judgment	Analysis of current skill	What is my analysis for improvement? How do I move forward to what I value?	
	-Effort	+Effort	What is a realistic view of the amount of effort required?	
	100 percent/0 percent performance	Any percent as something	On a continuum, where am I now with progress? What is realistic improvement?	
	Mistakes as catastrophes	Mistakes as opportunities	What may I learn from my mistake? What can I do differently?	
	Others as judges	Others as resources	Are they offering me useful, actionable information?	
	Competitive comparison	Constructive comparison	What may I learn from others? Is there something to be learned from their success?	

FM Emotions	FM Pattern	GM Pattern	Shift Questions	GM Emotions
(mild/moderate/intense)			How may I tolerate this? How do I calm myself?	

FM Behavior	FM Pattern	GM Pattern	Shift Questions	GM Behavior
	Choose too easy or very difficult tasks	Choose optimal challenges	How do I design a doable, step-by-step growth mindset plan? When will I start?	
	Decrease/hide effort	Increase efforts	How long will I stay with my plan (despite the effort)?	
	Excuses or exaggerations of progress	Accurate assessment of progress	What are my strengths and weaknesses? How do I move forward from weaknesses?	
	Hide mistakes	Analyze mistakes	What steps do I take to move forward from this mistake?	
	Seek those who praise and avoid critics	Seek critics who give helpful information	Who can give me helpful information? When will I use these resources?	
	Devalue/avoid successful others	Analysis of another's success	What steps have others taken to be successful? Can I take those steps?	

You can download copies of the growth mindset chart at http://www.newharbinger.com/48299 to work on your fixed mindset behaviors as well as your fixed mindset thoughts and emotions whenever you find yourself struggling with fixed mindset. The growth mindset chart can help you strengthen your growth mindset action plans.

Action plans take practice to develop and execute. If you find that you are not following through on your plan, ask yourself, "Are there fixed mindset thoughts that are getting in the way?" If so, talk back to them with growth mindset thoughts (see chapter 3). Additionally, ask yourself, "Is the first step of your plan realistic and doable? Can you visualize doing the very first step?" If not, it is not specific enough. Maybe you need to break it down into smaller tasks. Have you set aside a block of time to follow through with your plan? Think about your week, commit to a time to begin your plan. It may help to visualize executing the plan. As you do so, imagine experiencing some of the expected fixed mindset emotions; visualize following the plan despite these emotions (see chapter 4). Also, imagine the sense of mastery and pleasure when you complete your plan.

If you are having some difficulty coming up with an action plan, pretend that you are coaching a friend on how to develop a specific plan to move toward a valued goal. How would you help them to develop a growth mindset action plan? Consider that your friend needs a clear vision of what, when, and where to follow the plan.

Summary

Discouraging situations may jolt you into a fixed mindset, and without awareness, fixed mindset takes control and guides your actions. To stand firm against the fixed mindset, you need to recognize telltale reactions and use them as signposts to pivot to your growth mindset action plans. The following reactions are signs of a fixed mindset:

- When faced with a valued, challenging task, you choose an easy or extremely risky task; you procrastinate on challenging tasks.

- When a task feels effortful, you give up.

- When assessing your progress, you make positive exaggerations or excuses.

- When faced with mistakes, you hide mistakes from yourself and others.

- When faced with authorities who can give you feedback, you seek out those who praise and avoid those who criticize you.

- When hearing about the performance of peers, you denigrate or avoid peers whose performance is outstanding.

Recognize the above reactions and create your six-step growth mindset action plan despite feeling a bit apprehensive and avoidant. Use the growth mindset action plan worksheet to engage with:

- Moderately challenging activities

- More effort or persistence when a task is a struggle

- An accurate assessment of performance

- An analysis of mistakes

- Authorities who give critical but helpful feedback

- Peers who excel, examining their method for clues for improvement

Begin by practicing in a sphere that you somewhat value and create a growth mindset action plan to increase your skills. Then tackle the sphere that is more significant to you.

When trying out your action plan in an area that is extremely important to you, you may find it difficult to follow through on some of the six steps. Tackle the growth step that you dodge using a hierarchy.

Use the growth mindset chart to shift from fixed mindset to growth behaviors to strengthen your growth action plan.

CHAPTER 6

A Growth Mindset Chart to Keep You on Track

Growth mindset propels you toward what you value but is tough to sustain in light of disheartening experiences. Without awareness, fixed mindset entangles you in self-limiting thinking, mires you in unhelpful emotions, and narrows and restricts your choices. In earlier chapters, you learned how to identify the warning signs and to use special CBT tools to liberate you from this trap. With these tools you build the scaffolding upward to get back on the road toward a fulfilling life. You construct your escape platform with alternative growth mindset responses: coaching yourself with encouraging self-talk, climbing upward despite feeling pulled down by emotions, and taking steps forward, despite the urge to turn around because it feels risky.

It's challenging to simultaneously build up the different parts of your escape scaffolding. You need a blueprint to pull together all the pieces. The growth mindset chart is the blueprint: it assembles all the pieces with a coherent master plan.

Mastering the Growth Mindset Chart

In this chapter you'll become adept at following this blueprint. You'll use the chart to help others deal with growth mindset threat, learn from your own past growth mindset threats, and grapple with your future growth mindset threats.

Help Others Chart to a Growth Mindset

Sometimes the best way to become proficient at something is to tutor or coach someone else. This is especially true with the fixed mindset. Why is this? Have you had the experience of helping a friend or a family member deal with a disappointment—like the end of a relationship or a below-average report from a teacher? Although you felt empathy, you probably didn't feel the same intensity of disappointment that they experienced. Right? Did you notice that you were better able to counter some of the other person's negative thoughts—like "I'm a loser" or "I'm a failure"—than they were? Did you find that you were able to define some steps forward for them more readily than they could for themselves? Not experiencing the fixed mindset yourself can give you the calm and perspective that you need to help someone else. But in the end, what you learn from being the coach allows you to disentangle from your own fixed mindsets and regain your way.

Another example. Picture the common movie scene where the pilot of a plane becomes incapacitated and a passenger with no experience has to take over. So air traffic control turns over the radio headset to a flight instructor, who directs the understandably shaken passenger in how to land the plane. Put yourself in the shoes of the terrified passenger. Can you imagine that the passenger might have a fixed mindset? Beyond intense feelings, what might the passenger be thinking? Perhaps, *I can't do this* or *I don't know what to do.* The instructor remains cool and collected in the control tower, not feeling the same degree of horror.

What's the instructor's game plan? It's pretty complicated to fly a plane under any circumstances and especially if you have a fixed mindset. To assist the alarmed passenger with the three challenges of the fixed mindset, the instructor has to: counter thinking like *I can't do this,* reduce panic, and direct the passenger to take small steps despite their fear—essentially, help the passenger sustain a growth mindset about landing the plane. With the flight instructor's guidance, the frightened passenger maintains a growth mindset, makes an imperfect, bumpy landing, and saves the day.

The above scenario is way more extreme than you'll typically encounter when you try to tackle a fixed mindset and sustain a growth mindset. However, some time in your life, you may face an obstacle where the fixed mindset screams your survival is on the line. If this happens, shifting to a growth mindset will be critical for getting you to the other side. So let's practice the shift now when the stakes are lower.

Let's begin by coaching someone else who is struggling. Start by helping Jocelyn, a college sophomore, chart her way to a growth mindset. Imagine that she is a friend or family member. She has shared with you her trials at a very large university. She is a very dedicated student, working hard in all her classes with homework occupying most of her time. She is lonely, hasn't made any close friends, and misses her high school friends. She opts to try to join a sorority. She endures the intense process of interviewing with several sororities. She identifies one sorority as perfect for her. She calls you several weeks later—her first-choice sorority has rejected her.

Not only that. She also heard that her roommate, Ally, has been greenlighted by this same sorority. Although Jocelyn is accepted into her second-choice sorority, she expresses feelings of hurt, envy, and anger. She says, "How dare they reject me. Such a clique of princesses. They think they are so special. How could they accept Ally and not me! What's wrong with me—my sister had an easy time making friends in college. In the end, what matters is academics, and I am so much smarter than all of them! Who needs any of it?" She spends time on the call criticizing her preferred sorority and the sophomores that were accepted. She declares that she will not join any sorority.

Now maybe you can relate to Jocelyn and understand why she is so upset—or maybe not. Maybe you've never had an experience like this or ever been interested in joining a sorority. Regardless, it's unlikely that you're going to be upset the way she is or stuck with her self-limiting and vindictive thoughts. That's exactly the point. You are able to help Jocelyn because you have some perspective or distance from her experience. You can spy the telltale signs of the fixed mindset more easily than she can and tackle them by building a growth mindset scaffolding.

Let's start with some big-picture questions. What does Jocelyn really want? What was she looking for when she opted to join the sorority? What did she value? Was it friendships? What was her growth goal? It sounds like she wanted to make more friends, right? What is her obstacle to this goal? She's been rebuffed by her first-choice sorority. Have you ever had that experience where you wanted to be a part of a group, and that group didn't welcome you in? If so, how did you feel and respond? What is the fixed mindset that you may stumble into at that point? Could it be a shift from the growth mindset question of *How do I make friends?* to the fixed mindset question of *Am I popular or not?*

Use the growth mindset chart at http://www.newharbinger.com/48299 to capture all the signals of Jocelyn's fixed mindset. Write down Jocelyn's thoughts, feelings, and reactions in your downloaded copy. Circle the FM patterns that capture Jocelyn's FM thoughts and behaviors. Also circle the intensity of her emotions. Do you see how the fixed mindset is getting in the way of her social life? Now consider how you may help Jocelyn build a growth mindset scaffolding. The three components of this scaffolding are growth mindset thoughts, feelings, and actions. Build up each of these parts for Jocelyn. Again, reflect on the big picture of constructing a platform to break free of the fixed mindset—moving from judgments about adequacy to analysis for growth.

Look at the shift questions. They are prompts to help you generate some growth mindset responses. You may find some of the questions more relevant than others, yet it is helpful to read each one. Follow the prompts to help Jocelyn tackle her fixed mindset thoughts. Answer these questions as if you were Jocelyn. For example, how might you help her tackle her remarks about her sister? How might you help her tolerate or calm her emotions? Which of the techniques might she try? What action steps might she take? Use the shift questions for growth mindset behavior to come up with doable possibilities. Does she have other options on a college campus for meeting new friends?

Below is a completed version of Jocelyn's growth mindset chart. Compare it to yours. Is there anything you would change or add to your chart based on the comparison? Did you find some of Jocelyn's fixed mindset thoughts easier to shift than others? How about coming up with growth action steps? Some people find it easier to come up with growth mindset thoughts than growth actions steps; others not so much.

Jocelyn's Growth Mindset Chart

Describe your fixed mindset pothole: *Rejected from first-choice sorority*

Circle the type of pothole: (1) facing your challenging task; (2) experience of effort; (3) evaluating progress; (4) making a mistake; (5) praise or criticism; (6) the success or failure of others

[(5) praise or criticism and (6) the success or failure of others are circled]

FM Thoughts	FM Pattern	GM Pattern	Shift Questions	GM Thoughts
How dare they reject me. Such a clique of princesses. They think they are so special.	All-or-none self-judgment *(circled)*	Analysis of current skill	What is my analysis for improvement? How do I move forward to what I value?	This is disappointing, but doesn't mean that there is something wrong with them or me. Would love friends to hang with. That means being more comfortable with putting myself out there. How do I start to do that?
How could they accept Ally and not me!	-Effort *(circled)*	+Effort	What is a realistic view of the amount of effort required?	The other sorority is certainly a possibility. I did enjoy meeting some of the members there.
What's wrong with me? My sister had an easy time making friends in college!	100 percent/ 0 percent performance	Any percent as something	On a continuum, where am I now with progress? What is realistic improvement?	I've always liked singing – what about the choral group? Also, could join in some study groups that are meeting up at the commons.
In the end, what matters is academics and I am so much smarter than all of them!	Mistakes as catastrophes	Mistakes as opportunities	What may I learn from my mistake? What can I do differently?	Not everyone who rushed for this sorority got in. I did get into my second choice. What can I learn from this? Feeling angry is not going to make my social life better. Criticizing this sorority probably doesn't make me appealing. Stewing about something that I can't change won't help. What steps can I take to increase my chance of making new friends? Certainly, just focusing on my academics won't make that happen.
Who needs any of it!	Others as judges *(circled)*	Others as resources	Are they offering me useful, actionable information?	It is tough on such a large campus to connect with people, especially with all the homework I've had. I saw this sorority as an easy way to make some instant connections, but it takes some time and effort even with a sorority to find some people that I would like to hang with.
	Competitive comparison *(circled)*	Constructive comparison	What may I learn from others? Is there something to be learned from their success?	How did my sister make new friends in college? Maybe I could talk to her about her thoughts and what worked for her.

FM Emotions	FM Pattern	GM Pattern	Shift Questions	GM Emotions
(mild/moderate/intense)			How may I tolerate this? How do I calm myself?	
Hurt, envy, anger			Deep breathing. Here-and-now focusing. FLOAT	Somewhat hopeful, determined

FM Behavior	FM Pattern	GM Pattern	Shift Questions	GM Behavior
Criticize Ally and sorority. Avoid joining second-choice sorority. Focus on academics. Give up on making new friends	Choose too easy or very difficult tasks	Choose optimal challenges	How do I design a doable, step-by-step growth mindset plan? When will I start?	Give the second-choice sorority a chance by going out with some of its members for coffee. Text Jan to meet for coffee.
	Decrease/hide effort	Increase efforts	How long will I stay with my plan (despite the effort)?	Check out the choral group on Wednesday.
	Excuses or exaggerations of progress	Accurate assessment of progress	What are my strengths and weaknesses? How do I move forward from weaknesses?	Look at the listing of study groups in commons.
	Hide mistakes	Analyze mistakes	What steps do I take to move forward from this mistake?	Call sister this weekend to find out how she met her college friends.
	Seek those who give praise and avoid critics	Seek critics who give helpful information	Who can give me helpful information? When will I use these resources?	
	Devalue/avoid successful others	Analysis of another's success	What steps have others taken to be successful? Can I take those steps?	

Let's turn to another example: see what you may do to help your friend Julio chart his way to a growth mindset. Six months ago, Julio lost his job as an accountant, a position that he had held for nine years. He enjoyed this job and felt he was contributing to his team and the company. During a turn in the economy, however, the company downsized and laid off Julio and his colleague Fab. Unemployment has not been easy for Julio. His wife works as a special ed teacher, but even with unemployment benefits, it has been a struggle to meet the bills and mortgage payments, plus all the expenses involved with raising two young boys. He's been going to a job-seekers meeting at the local YMCA and reaching out to everyone he knows for possible job leads. Since his layoff, he has not contacted Fab, although they were friendly during their years together.

One night, Julio calls you—clearly upset—he has missed a deadline for a web-posted job opening. He shares that he is irritated with himself for having lost the last two days gaming on the internet. He says, "What an idiot I am. Not organized enough. I can't believe I missed this deadline. I'll never get a job if I can't handle something as simple as this. I heard from my wife that Fab has had many interviews. This would never happen to him!"

Let's analyze what's happening with Julio by starting with some questions. What was Julio's growth goal, and what was the obstacle that threw him off track? Did his mistake jolt him into a fixed mindset? Do you have evidence that before this mistake he was pretty much on track in strengthening his job-finding skills? What are the specific skills that Julio needs to find a job, and are there any skills that he needs to beef up?

Have you ever had that experience where you slipped up while trying to achieve something that was important to you? If so, how did you feel and respond? What is the fixed mindset that you may fall into at that point? Could it be a shift from the growth mindset question of *How do I recover and build the skill to move forward?* to the fixed mindset conclusion of *I'm incompetent?*

Use another growth mindset chart at http://www.newharbinger.com/48299 to fill in all the information that signals Julio's fixed mindset. Write down Julio's thoughts, emotions, and actions in the downloaded chart. Circle the FM patterns that capture Julio's FM thoughts and behaviors, and circle the intensity of his emotions. Do you see how Julio's fixed mindset is getting in the way of job hunting? How can you help Julio construct a growth mindset scaffolding? Zoom out and consider how you would help him move from judgments about adequacy to analysis for growth. Follow the prompts in the shift questions to tackle his fixed mindset thoughts. Answer these questions as if you were Julio. For example, what is the specific problem to address using the growth mindset thinking? What would he specifically like to improve? How might you help him tolerate or calm his emotions? Which of the techniques might he try? What action steps might he take? Use the shift questions for growth mindset behavior to come up with doable possibilities.

Compare your chart for Julio to this completed version of his growth mindset chart. Is there anything you would change or add to your chart based on comparison? Did you find some of Julio's thoughts easier to shift than others? Consider the growth action steps. Are there some actions that Julio may find more difficult to take than others—how about contacting Fab?

Julio's Growth Mindset Chart

Describe your fixed mindset pothole: *Missing a job web-posted deadline*

Circle the type of pothole: (1) facing your challenging task; (2) experience of effort; (3) evaluating progress; (4) making a mistake; (5) praise or criticism; (6) the success or failure of others

FM Thoughts	FM Pattern	GM Pattern	Shift Questions	GM Thoughts
What an idiot I am. Not organized enough.	All-or-none self-judgment	Analysis of current skill	What is my analysis for improvement? How do I move forward to what I value?	I would like to get another accounting job. I enjoyed my previous job and the contribution that I made.
I can't believe I missed this deadline.	-Effort	+Effort	What is a realistic view of the amount of effort required?	Finding a job is a difficult task. I have not done a job search for a number of years, and a lot has changed. The economy is worse. I am trying to manage my bills including my mortgage payments.
I'll never get a job if I can't handle something as simple as this.	100 percent/ 0 percent performance	Any percent as something	On a continuum, where am I now with progress? What is realistic improvement?	It is not easy to be as organized as I would like under these circumstances.
Fab has had so many interviews. This would never happen to him!	Mistakes as catastrophes	Mistakes as opportunities	What may I learn from my mistake? What can I do differently?	I missed the deadline for the web-posted job. I would like to get more organized.
	Others as judges	Others as resources	Are they offering me useful, actionable information?	I read about this job months ago. The deadline seemed far away and I didn't put it in my calendar. I was also on the fence about the job because it didn't seem perfect for me. In the future, when I see a job posting that is of interest but may not be perfect, I will put the deadline into my calendar immediately and set up some alerts. I can always decide later not to apply, or I can apply and see what happens.
	Competitive comparison	Constructive comparison	What may I learn from others? Is there something to be learned from their success?	There is a job-seekers group that meets at the YMCA. Maybe I can attend and see what ideas they may have for getting more organized. Fab is a good friend. Maybe I could talk to him about his ways of keeping organized.

FM Emotions	FM Pattern	GM Pattern	Shift Questions	GM Emotions
	(mild/moderate/(intense))		How may I tolerate this? How do I calm myself?	
Irritated at self			Deep breathing. Here-and-now focusing. FLOAT	Somewhat hopeful, more determined

FM Behavior	FM Pattern	GM Pattern	Shift Questions	GM Behavior
Gaming on the internet	(Choose too easy or very difficult tasks)	Choose optimal challenges	How do I design a doable, step-by-step growth mindset plan? When will I start?	Call YMCA tomorrow when it opens.
	(Decrease/hide effort)	Increase efforts	How long will I stay with my plan (despite the effort)?	Call Fab tonight.
	Excuses or exaggerations of progress	Accurate assessment of progress	What are my strengths and weaknesses? How do I move forward from weaknesses?	Review postings on websites this week during the day and practice putting deadlines into calendar with alerts.
	Hide mistakes	Analyze mistakes	What steps do I take to move forward from this mistake?	
	Seek those who praise and avoid critics	Seek critics who give helpful information	Who can give me helpful information? When will I use these resources?	
	Devalue/avoid successful others	Analysis of another's success	What steps have others taken to be successful? Can I take those steps?	

Sometimes it can be difficult to make the mindset shift in yourself. You can, however, become better at it by asking how you would coach someone else into a growth mindset. Think about someone you know who may be yearning to learn something new or get better at something unfamiliar and is encountering a growth menace. Are there any telltale signs of a fixed mindset? What would you say to reinforce growth mindset? How would you accept and help them let go of fixed mindset emotions? What growth mindset behaviors would you encourage?

Help a Younger You Chart to a Growth Mindset

How did growth and fixed mindset impact the younger you? Time can give you some perspective on these mindsets and reinforce your growth mindset of today. Start by creating a timeline of your life in increments of five years—zero to five, six to ten, eleven to fifteen. Leave out the last ten years to gain some distance and more perspective.

Reflect on Your Younger Mindsets

Reflect on your life within the five-year blocks on your timeline. For each period of time, do you recall trying to get better at something specific that was important to you? What was it? An example might be: zero to age five, *learn to tie sneakers,* or six to ten, *ride a bike.* How about the later blocks? Get better at a sport or a musical instrument? What about becoming more engaged with friends or family or developing a close relationship with someone?

_____

_____

_____

_____

_____

_____

Did you sustain your growth mindset despite setbacks? For example, did you fall off your two-wheeler, when you made the mistake of steering too sharply, and then get back on and keep riding? Write about any experiences where you thrived despite setbacks.

_____

_____

_____

_____

Did you start out with a growth mindset and become ensnared in a fixed mindset after a setback? For example, when you did not make the cut for middle-school orchestra, did you give up playing your instrument? When the love of your life in high school broke it off with you, did you back off dating for two years? Write about any experiences where your growth to recovery was delayed (shaky or prolonged).

_____

_____

Most people recall a mix of experiences when faced with obstacles. Select two from your past life—one experience where you thrived despite the setback and one experience where your recovery to the growth path was delayed.

For me, an early memory of facing an obstacle was at the age of ten: a suburban child visiting my grandmother's farm in the summer for two weeks, heading out to the pasture to corral and ride my cousins' ponies. Me with no experience in riding but determined. Cousins saddle up the ponies. I choose a pinto, Diablo (his name should have been a clue).

Despite some harrowing moments, being bucked off into a barbed-wire fence and many scratches and bruises, I hung on, rode every day, and was better at riding at the end of my stay. I continued to strengthen my equestrian skills well into my fifties.

Another setback in my life with a much shakier recovery: in my late twenties, in graduate school in social psychology, I failed my qualifying exams (needed to proceed to a thesis). Shook me to the core. Felt defeated and questioned whether or not I had what it takes to get a PhD. Compared myself to everyone else who passed, and questioned whether I measured up. My first impulse was to avoid everyone in the department—feeling embarrassed. Considered dropping out. It took several weeks to regain my footing. Eventually I moved forward: did an analysis of my exam, consulted with peers and professors, studied more, took the exam a second time, and passed it. Ultimately, I finished my degree, and here I am writing this book about both experiences.

Look at the two situations that you've chosen from your own past: one experience where you thrived despite a setback and the other where your recovery to growth was delayed. Take some time to write about these experiences in your journal or in a notebook. For each, remember that moment when you were stretching yourself and experienced a setback. What were you doing? Where were you? Were you alone or with others? What was happening around you? What did you say to yourself? How did you feel? How did you respond? Now compare and contrast the two situations. How were your responses different?

Use the growth mindset chart at http://www.newharbinger.com/48299 for the instance where your recovery was delayed. Retrospectively write down the signs of a fixed mindset on your chart. Also, capture any growth mindset challenges or steps that you spontaneously may have taken back then to help yourself get back on track. Now look at the prompts. As the older you who encourages and coaches the younger you into a growth mindset, is there anything else you would add or change on the chart? Any additional suggestions for challenging self-limiting thoughts, calming emotions, or taking additional actions steps?

Remember that sometimes past fixed mindsets are very difficult to change. If you are mired or stuck in a particular fixed mindset from your past, share it with someone who may be able to help, like a close friend, family member, or even a professional. Find someone like the instructor in the control tower who by virtue of their distance from your lived experience or training can assist you in navigating back.

Help an Older You Chart to a Growth Mindset

What growth mindset threats may lie in wait for the older you? Considering them now can help you prepare for them, much like a pilot prepares for potential air catastrophes by training in a flight simulator. The simulated catastrophe like the loss of an engine is realistic, alarming, and jarring but never as terrifying as the actual experience. Such training allows the pilot to sustain and build skills despite threats that understandably could provoke a fixed mindset: *Am I competent or not?*

Remember Sully Sullenberger? He was the pilot who managed to land a jet in the Hudson River saving all 155 passengers, despite losing two engines. How did he accomplish this? He certainly never practiced landing a passenger plane on the Hudson. Is it that some people are heroes and some are not? Are some people strong and some weak? When the flock of birds destroyed his engines, did Sullenberger make a global judgment about his competence, like *I'm an amazing pilot,* or did he do an analysis focused on how to land the plane, refining and honing his skills as the crisis unfolded? Although you can never predict what life may throw at you, you can prepare by exposing yourself to the what-if growth menaces that may bar your way to a fulfilling life. How can you train yourself to cope with potential threats to what you desire?

To train for future growth menaces, you need a menace simulator, just as a pilot has a flight simulator for potential air catastrophes. You will build your growth menace simulator with your imagination and your growth mindset chart. First, you imagine taking steps toward something significant to you: maybe it's a new career or a new relationship. Next, you conjure up your most fearsome growth menace as you move down that path with your growth mindset. Then you capture that scenario on the growth mindset chart, with a vivid accounting of your feelings, thoughts, and actions when you face that challenge.

Imagined Worst-Case Scenario

Let's return to the story of Alexandra, who has taken some risky growth steps toward her goal of finding a long-term relationship: putting herself out there by posting a profile online, letting friends and family know she is interested in meeting people, and even asking an attractive man to join her for coffee after the environmental group meeting. What's the worst she could imagine as she continues to stretch herself? Alexandra reflects, *Meet someone whom I adore and then, after several years of being in an exclusive relationship, he breaks up with me.* Although Alexandra never has been in a relationship longer than two months, this is her worst-case scenario setback and what she will address on her growth mindset chart.

Now here is where an even more developed imagination comes in. Alexandra produces the movie version of the breakup. In this movie version, she is the director as well as the heroine. The heroine adores this man and is committed forever after. He is everything she has dreamed of and more. Then—one night over dinner at their favorite restaurant when she thought they were about to discuss moving into an apartment together—he becomes dead serious and proclaims, "Not happening for me. Let's call it quits. Maybe we can be friends at some other point?" Not to make light of what would be crushing for anyone who actually sees their future unraveling.

The point is that this is all make-believe, which makes it easier to have perspective: Alexandra has never been in a long-term relationship; she has not met the guy of her dreams or experienced any incredible times with him. This is an exercise to build your resilience. For it to be effective, the imagined scenario, like the flight simulator, must be vivid and feel alarming, upsetting, and scary. So imagining the worst-case scenario of her relationship future, Alexandra crafts a very compelling scene for herself, enters into it, immerses herself in it, and then asks, *What might I think? How would I feel? What would I do?* and writes plausible responses to these questions into her growth mindset chart. Additionally, Alexandra asks herself, *Might I suddenly tumble into the fixed mindset, asking a question like, Am I lovable or unlovable? If so, what would be the signs?* Alexander captures those telltale patterns on the growth mindset chart.

Then, stepping back as the director, Alexandra considers, *How do I help the heroine recover from this scene using the growth mindset prompts? How would I help her weather this breakup? What might I say? How do I help her tolerate the pain, loss, and humiliation? What growth action steps would I recommend, so she can rebound from this rejection and continue to put herself out there?* Here is Alexandra's growth mindset chart with the fixed mindset responses of the heroine. Can you complete the chart as the director of the movie, helping her to create her growth mindset responses? Fill in GM thoughts for Alexandra in response to the shift questions in the chart.

Alexandra's Growth Mindset Chart: Imagined Worst-Case Scenario

Describe your fixed mindset pothole: *After several years, the man of my dreams breaks up with me*

Circle the type of pothole: (1) facing your challenging task; (2) experience of effort; (3) evaluating progress; (4) making a mistake; (5) praise or criticism; (6) the success or failure of others

FM Thoughts	FM Pattern	GM Pattern	Shift Questions	GM Thoughts
I can't believe it. What a jerk! He thinks I'm not good enough for him.	All-or-none self-judgment	Analysis of current skill	What is my analysis for improvement? How do I move forward to what I value?	
He's found someone better—someone more interesting and more attractive than me.	-Effort	+Effort	What is a realistic view of the amount of effort required?	
How stupid I am. Should have seen this coming.	100 percent/ 0 percent performance	Any percent as something	On a continuum, where am I now with progress? What is realistic improvement?	
Can't believe I wasted these years on him.	Mistakes as catastrophes	Mistakes as opportunities	What may I learn from my mistake? What can I do differently?	
What's the point? Never will find someone who's happy with me	Others as judges	Others as resources	Are they offering me useful, actionable information?	
	Competitive comparison	Constructive comparison	What may I learn from others? Is there something to be learned from their success?	

FM Emotions	FM Pattern	GM Pattern	Shift Questions	GM Emotions
(mild/moderate/intense)			How may I tolerate this? How do I calm myself?	
Hurt, confused, embarrassed, devastated			Deep breathing. Here-and-now focusing. FLOAT.	

FM Behavior	FM Pattern	GM Pattern	Shift Questions	GM Behavior
Go out with guys she's not that into. Guys who like her more than she likes them.	Choose too easy or very difficult tasks	Choose optimal challenges	How do I design a doable, step-by-step growth mindset plan? When will I start?	
Doesn't share details with close friends or family, tells them breakup was mutual.	Decrease/hide effort	Increase efforts	How long will I stay with my plan (despite the effort)?	
Avoids contact with mutual friends, especially couples who seems to be happy together.	Excuses or exaggerations of progress	Accurate assessment of progress	What are my strengths and weaknesses? How do I move forward from weaknesses?	
	Hide mistakes	Analyze mistakes	What steps do I take to move forward from this mistake?	
Tells her friends that he really was a jerk. Just another man whom you can't trust.	Seek those who praise and avoid critics	Seek critics who give helpful information	Who can give me helpful information? When will I use these resources?	
	Devalue/avoid successful others	Analysis of another's success	What steps have others taken to be successful? Can I take those steps?	

As you predict what potholes may lie ahead, keep in mind that they may be camouflaged as something seemingly positive. Consider the same breakup but from the point of view of Alexandra's partner. Imagine yourself as the object of Alexandra's adoration. Your partner thinks you walk on water, and you believe it. How might that view of yourself get in the way of sustaining a relationship that adapts to the challenges of living with someone?

Imagined Best-Case Scenario

Let's use the menace simulator with a best-case scenario. This is an exercise to build resilience to seemingly positive events that might undercut your growth mindset. Return to Marcel from chapter 5, who has developed a landscaping business. He has stretched himself, managing a new bookkeeper and a foreman. This gives him more time to develop advertising and respond to customer inquiries and make estimates for projects. He's made enough money to afford some additional equipment. For this exercise, he asks, *What's the best-case scenario for my business? Being wildly successful and doing so well that my biggest competitor closes.*

Next, he creates a vivid movie version of the scene and immerses himself in it. This is his winning-the-lottery version of his business: His advertising campaign is amazingly successful with new customers calling and emailing daily. His business signs appear on the lawns of every upscale neighborhood. His equipment is top of the line. His very large crew is competent and professional, and all reviews online are five stars. Then he hears the news: his biggest competitor has folded, filing for bankruptcy. Sounds great? Right?

He puts himself into that scene and asks, *What are my thoughts, feelings, and actions when I hear about my competitor failing?* He asks, *Could this seemingly positive scene be a trigger for a fixed mindset? How would I know?* He captures the thoughts, feelings, and actions that would signal a fixed mindset on the following chart. Can you complete the chart, building his scaffolding of growth mindset responses? Fill in GM thoughts for Marcel in response to the shift questions in the chart.

Marcel's Growth Mindset Chart: Imagined Best-Case Scenario

Describe your fixed mindset pothole: *Hearing that my biggest competitor is going out of business*

Circle the type of pothole: (1) facing your challenging task; (2) experience of effort; (3) evaluating progress; (4) making a mistake; (5) praise or criticism; (6) the success or failure of others

FM Thoughts	FM Pattern	GM Pattern	Shift Questions	GM Thoughts
I'm king around here. He was such a lightweight.	All-or-none self-judgment	Analysis of current skill	What is my analysis for improvement? How do I move forward to what I value?	
	-Effort	+Effort	What is a realistic view of the amount of effort required?	
	100 percent/0 percent performance	Any percent as something	On a continuum, where am I now with progress? What is realistic improvement?	
	Mistakes as catastrophes	Mistakes as opportunities	What may I learn from my mistake? What can I do differently?	
	Others as judges	Others as resources	Are they offering me useful, actionable information?	
	Competitive comparison	Constructive comparison	What may I learn from others? Is there something to be learned from their success?	

FM Emotions	FM Pattern	GM Pattern	Shift Questions	GM Emotions
(mild ⟨moderate⟩ intense)			How may I tolerate this? How do I calm myself?	
Gloat			*Deep breathing. Here-and-now focusing. FLOAT*	

FM Behavior	FM Pattern	GM Pattern	Shift Questions	GM Behavior
Pull back from customer outreach	Choose too easy or very difficult tasks	Choose optimal challenges	How do I design a doable, step-by-step growth mindset plan? When will I start?	
Decrease advertising budget and overspend on new truck	Decrease/hide effort	Increase efforts	How long will I stay with my plan (despite the effort)?	
Spend more time playing golf and less time meeting and supervising crews	Excuses or exaggerations of progress	Accurate assessment of progress	What are my strengths and weaknesses? How do I move forward from weaknesses?	
	Hide mistakes	Analyze mistakes	What steps do I take to move forward from this mistake?	
Brag to friends and family about how successful I am and what a loser my competitor was	Seek those who praise and avoid critics	Seek critics who give helpful information	Who can give me helpful information? When will I use these resources?	
	Devalue/avoid successful others	Analysis of another's success	What steps have others taken to be successful? Can I take those steps?	

Note that I am not suggesting that your victories deserve no celebration. I'm not suggesting that Marcel immediately put his nose to the grindstone. I'm just saying, beware when a victory turns into a fixed mindset threat that undermines growth responses that sustain and build what's important to you.

What growth menace lies in wait for a future you? Choose an area in your life satisfaction questionnaire from chapter 2 where you have made some progress, such as improving your health through exercise. Consider a worst-case scenario growth menace that may lie in your future: your physician indicating that despite your exercise, you have severe coronary heart disease (*I'm powerless*). Now consider a best-case scenario menace that may lie in your future: your physician indicating your physiological age is like that of someone ten years your junior (*I'm invincible!*).

Create two vivid and compelling movie scenes in which you confront your worst- and best-case growth menaces. Put yourself in both movies. Imagine your responses to each of these scenarios. Experience that moment: what would you feel, think, and do? Might you tumble into a fixed mindset? What would be the indicators of the fixed mindset? Use your imagination and growth mindset charts available at http://www.newharbinger.com/48299 to foretell fixed mindset reactions and plan your growth mindset defenses. Use one chart to imagine your worst scenario and another chart to imagine your best scenario. Practicing this will build your resilience to future fixed mindset threats.

Summary

Fixed mindset entangles you in self-limiting thinking, mires you in unhelpful emotions, and narrows your choices. Defy these three fixed mindset snares and strengthen your growth mindset through mastering the growth mindset chart:

- Coach someone else into a growth mindset using the growth mindset chart as your guide.

- Coach a younger you into a growth mindset—relive a challenging setback from your past, and use the growth mindset chart to let go of it and restructure it.

- Coach an older you into a growth mindset—imagine a growth menace in your future, and use the growth mindset chart to build resilience.

With the growth mindset chart as your blueprint, you construct your fixed mindset escape platform: coaching yourself with encouraging self-talk, climbing upward despite feeling pulled down by emotions, and taking steps forward, despite the urge to turn around because going forward feels risky.

PART 2

Applying a Growth Mindset

CHAPTER 7

A Growth Mindset to Promote Professional Goals

Growth mindset can propel you toward a professional life that you value, but it is tough to sustain in light of the many obstacles you may face while building your skills, creating your resume, applying for jobs, encountering competitive markets, conducting interviews, developing customers, and networking. Without awareness, fixed mindset can sidetrack your professional growth: entangle you in career-limiting thinking, distract you with unhelpful emotions, and narrow and restrict your occupational options. In previous chapters, you've learned to identify the warning signs of the fixed mindset and to use special CBT tools to liberate you from this trap. In this chapter, you'll use these tools to build the scaffolding upward to get back on the road toward a more fulfilling work life. You'll construct your platform with alternative growth mindset responses: coaching yourself with career enhancing self-talk, climbing upward toward your professional goal, letting go of limiting emotions, and taking steps forward despite the urge to stay where you are in your current job because it feels safe.

This chapter will help you if you value developing your career and are dissatisfied with your professional life: you rated your satisfaction as 0 or below on your life satisfaction questionnaire (see chapter 2). In this chapter we'll apply what you've learned about the growth mindset to your professional development. There are some great books on developing your career and finding jobs. It's not easy to develop your career, so I recommend doing some outside reading to support you in this quest.

The growth mindset chart is your career development blueprint. It assembles all the pieces with a master plan to sustain your growth mindset. In this chapter, you will:

1. Unpack your professional dissatisfaction and turn it into a professional growth goal.

2. Visualize a step toward that professional goal and commit to it.

3. Use the growth mindset chart and your CBT tools to detect and defend against the six growth mindset menaces that may hamper your professional progress.

After you complete the first step, you will take the second concrete step toward your professional goal, watch out, and fend off growth menaces, and repeat. Take one step at a time, maintaining your growth mindset with your CBT skills as you go.

Turn Your Career Dissatisfaction into Professional Goals

How do you turn career dissatisfaction into a growth goal? Let's illustrate by looking at Gerri, who feels trapped in her job. She has worked as a data analyst in an insurance firm. She's been there for three years and has great performance reviews. She likes data analytics, but her department is understaffed and she is working overtime on weekdays and weekends to meet project deadlines. Her pleas to her supervisor for additional personnel and a raise go unheeded. Gerri feels stuck. She tells herself she should apply for jobs in another industry or company, but she can't even find the time to exercise. She finds herself working late, coming home exhausted, and falling asleep streaming her favorite TV series. Then she does the same thing the next day. This is how the last three years have passed. Can you use what you have learned from this book to help Gerri? Where would you start? What does fixed mindset have to do with this?

Sometimes it is not easy to figure out how you would like to grow in your professional life. That's to be expected, especially if you have been caught up in a fixed mindset. A fixed mindset is limiting in that you restrict yourself to situations where you feel safe but dissatisfied. For example, Gerri is unhappy with her work but feels she doesn't have the energy to change it. How do you escape this trap and develop your professional life?

Identify Specific Areas of Dissatisfaction in Your Work

Ask yourself the following questions:

1. In what ways are you dissatisfied with your professional life?

    _____

2. Is your dissatisfaction something about the work you do? For example, are you bored with tasks of the job? Are there some tasks that you dislike more than others? Write out your specific dissatisfactions about your work tasks here:

    _____

3. Is your dissatisfaction something about the work environment: not enough support, not enough compensation, not enough balance, not enough human interaction or too much human interaction? Write out your specific dissatisfactions about your work environment here:

_____

Now turn your dissatisfaction into a professional growth goal by asking the following questions:

- Are there professional activities that you think may be interesting but have avoided out of concern for failing or looking foolish?

- Are there professional areas that you value and think you might be good at, but you've avoided them and avoided stretching yourself because you don't want to find out that you're not?

- Are there professional activities that feel safe but boring? These may be activities where you feel confident that you can show yourself to be competent (or even talented), but perhaps you find that you're a bit weary of them. What professional activities may be more fun or interesting but feel a bit risky?

- Are there some professional changes that you've tried to make but became frustrated and then gave up? Would you value these professional changes if you felt you could make them with little effort?

- Were there times in your professional life when you felt challenged and excited about learning something new? What activity were you engaged in? Can you still feel that excitement? Can you feel that excitement (along with some natural trepidations) as you contemplate something new? What were the aspects of the earlier activity that you enjoyed? Is there a similar activity now that you may engage in?

Gerri asks herself these questions and concludes that she would love to have a job in another company where she felt she could be part of a team. She once had an internship in a company where management promoted a team approach. She felt excited by the interactions and energized when she made contributions to the work group. She likes what she does—she likes data analytics—but she dislikes the isolation in her work environment. She would apply for jobs in other companies if it did not require so much effort.

In short, Gerri turns her dissatisfaction into a growth goal, asking herself, *What would I do if I weren't concerned about failing, playing it safe, or looking bad? What would I do if I could do it with little effort?* Here is Gerri's professional growth goal: *Find a job in a company that fosters a team environment.*

What about you? What is your professional growth goal? If you are bored or dissatisfied with your work, how would you challenge yourself if you weren't concerned with failing? Would you take an online course? Go back to school? Find a mentor? Ask for a promotion? If you weren't concerned with playing it safe, would you want to take on more professional responsibility? For example, would you seek out more management opportunities? If you weren't concerned with looking bad, would you seek another position in the same or in a different company or in a different industry? If you thought you could do so with little effort, would you consider a job in a different geographic location? Would you consider starting your own business?

Remember, a professional growth goal may excite you even though when you consider it you get scared, feel avoidant, and perhaps fear failing. Choose a professional goal where stretching yourself would increase your satisfaction.

Write your professional growth goal here: _____

Visualize a Step Toward Your Goal and Commit to It

Now that you have a professional growth goal, what first small step could you take to move toward it? Can you imagine or visualize taking that small step? If not, ask yourself is there a small step that you would need to take prior to that step? Visualize taking that small step at a specific point in time. It needs to be something that makes you feel moderately uncomfortable or a bit uneasy.

To illustrate, here is Gerri's process. At first she believes her first small step is to research promising companies. She tries to visualize taking that step and committing to it. Then she realizes that to do this research she needs to make time during her week. She is exhausted and stressed from working overtime and on the weekends, so can't imagine having the energy to move forward in her career. She comes to appreciate that her first small step is actually to set limits on the hours that she devotes to work so that she can de-stress enough to devote time to her growth goal.

Gerri's first small step is to quit work at 5:30 and not 6 p.m. two times a week, so she can carve out time to exercise for half an hour. She feels uneasy about leaving work at 5:30 two days each week, but she can visualize leaving work, doing a half-hour on her exercise bike.

Gerri organizes her plan using the growth goal worksheet from chapter 2. Here is what she came up with:

Growth goal: *Find a job in a company that fosters a team environment.*

First small step: *Set limits at work, so I can exercise on bike and have energy for growth goal.*

Even-though feeling: *Concerned my coworkers will look down on me*

Schedule step on calendar: *Monday and Wednesday leave work at 5 pm. Exercise bike 5:30 to 6 p.m.*

What about you? What first small step could you take toward your professional goal—a concrete step that you can imagine taking at a specific point during your week and that makes you a bit uncomfortable?

Taking Your First Small Step

Write your responses to the prompts below:

First small step: What first small step could you take to begin to develop your professional life?

_____

_____

Even-though feeling: Describe what makes you a bit uneasy about taking that small step. It may be a thought or a feeling. What exactly is making you apprehensive or uncomfortable?

_____

If you can visualize that step, then commit to taking it despite your discomfort.

Schedule the step on your calendar: Write it down. This can be a physical calendar or your phone, wherever you are most likely to see it and take action.

Gerri finds that although she's uneasy about leaving work early for exercise, she eventually makes doing this part of her routine. Setting some limits with work, so she has more energy, is just a first step in Gerri's quest to develop a career aligned with what she values. There are many more steps to take after that, and for Gerri, some of these steps prove to be more difficult than step one.

Detect and Defend Against Six Professional Growth Menaces

So far, none of this sounds so hard to do, right? Unpacking your dissatisfaction on the job and turning it into a growth goal; visualizing a step toward that goal and committing to it—sounds straightforward, right? It's simply about filling out the growth goal worksheet.

Who hasn't decided to go for a growth goal, say to improve your health? You commit to a step and schedule it in your calendar: get on the exercise bike Mondays and Wednesdays, 5:30 to 6 p.m.? Easy, right? For some people maybe, but for others not so much. Why? The answer is, it may not be easy, but that's okay—it's about maintaining your growth mindset.

You know from reading this book that the big challenge lies with detecting and defending against the fixed mindset as you take each of the small steps toward your growth goals. You watch out for that wall of fixed mindset thoughts, emotions, and actions that you slam into as you try to improve your health, your relationships, or your career. Then you build your growth mindset scaffolding to climb over it.

Remember that sometimes you don't recognize you've smashed into a wall. The wall confines you, and you just live within it. Everything seems okay and safe. But is it? How do you know?

Is this the life that you value within these walls? Or, if you were not concerned with failing, looking foolish, making mistakes, playing it safe, would you put in the effort, climb out, and go for something else?

Watch out for the six growth menaces, and use your special CBT skills to detect fixed mindset and maintain your growth mindset defenses to complete the concrete steps.

Back to Gerri, what growth menaces might she encounter as she pursues her professional goals? Your task is to coach Gerri through the steps needed to make a career move: research companies, revise her resume, network, conduct informational interviews, go to job interviews. Help her to maintain a growth mindset through each of these steps, detecting and defending against the growth mindset obstacles that she is likely to encounter. Through coaching Gerri, you'll increase your resilience to the disheartening situations you'll face as you develop your own career.

Researching Companies

So let's start with an obstacle Gerri encounters as she takes steps to research companies online. She has scheduled time on Saturday and Sunday morning between 10 and 11 a.m. after breakfast to do this. She sits down at her computer at 10 a.m. on Saturday to research companies for one hour. After struggling a bit trying to vet companies, she looks at the time. It's 10:47. She feels frustrated and says to herself, *I've spent forty-seven minutes and have nothing, not one promising company! I'm a data analyst. It shouldn't be this hard! Alisha found a new job she likes in less than a month. What's wrong with me? At this pace, I'll never find what I'm looking for. Even if I do find an opening, they won't be interested in hiring me.*

Gerri jumps up from her computer and starts a load of laundry, then texts a friend to meet up for lunch. What happened? What fixed mindset potholes has Gerri encountered? What patterns do you see in her thoughts? What is the shift in her emotions—what is she feeling? What about her reactions? See if you can detect Gerri's fixed mindset thoughts, feelings, and actions and capture them on the growth mindset chart (available at http://www.newharbinger.com/48299).

Now how would Gerri handle this process if she were able to sustain a growth mindset? Can you help Gerri build a growth mindset scaffolding? How would you encourage her with growth mindset self-talk? How would you help her let go of her feelings of frustration? What might you suggest when she experiences these feelings? What growth mindset actions might you suggest?

Complete the professional growth mindset chart for Gerri. Now take a look at this example of how it may be completed.

Gerri's Professional Growth Mindset Chart: Researching Companies

Describe your fixed mindset pothole: *Researching companies on my computer on Saturday for forty-seven minutes*

Circle the type of pothole: (1) facing your challenging task; (2) experience of effort; (3) evaluating progress; (4) making a mistake; (5) praise or criticism; (6) the success or failure of others

FM Thoughts	FM Pattern	GM Pattern	Shift Questions	GM Thoughts
I've spent forty-seven minutes and have nothing! I'm a data analyst. It shouldn't be this hard!	All-or-none self-judgment	Analysis of current skill	What is my analysis for improvement? How do I move forward to what I value?	I have been working on this for forty-seven minutes. It will take some time to do the research on companies.
Alisha found a new job she likes in less than a month. What's wrong with me?	-Effort	+Effort	What is a realistic view of the amount of effort required?	It would be great if I could find the perfect company after doing this for forty-seven minutes, but it's not probable.
I'll never find what I'm looking for.	100 percent/0 percent performance	Any percent as something	On a continuum, where am I now with progress? What is realistic improvement?	I am really just learning how to do this type of research. So it's expected that my first attempt will go slowly. Just because I'm good at my job doesn't mean I'm good at everything. Are there some resources out there? Do I know of someone else who may have done this type of research? Could I talk to Alisha?
	Mistakes as catastrophes	Mistakes as opportunities	What may I learn from my mistake? What can I do differently?	
Even if I do find an opening, they won't be interested in hiring me.	Others as judges	Others as resources	Are they offering me useful, actionable information?	
	Competitive comparison	Constructive comparison	What may I learn from others? Is there something to be learned from their success?	I'm getting ahead of myself by making predictions about if I'll be hired. Let me just stick with my plan to do the research.

FM Emotions	FM Pattern	GM Pattern	Shift Questions	GM Emotions
(mild/moderate/intense)			How may I tolerate this? How do I calm myself?	
Frustration			Deep breathing. FLOAT.	Less frustrated, more focused

FM Behavior	FM Pattern	GM Pattern	Shift Questions	GM Behavior
Jump up. Start laundry. Call a friend about meeting up for lunch. Avoid doing research on Sunday.	Choose too easy or very difficult tasks	Choose optimal challenges	How do I design a doable, step-by-step growth mindset plan? When will I start?	Sit at computer for one hour regardless of feelings. Do this again on Sunday.
	Decrease/hide effort	Increase efforts	How long will I stay with my plan (despite the effort)?	Look at books and other resources that deal with vetting company climate.
	Excuses or exaggerations of progress	Accurate assessment of progress	What are my strengths and weaknesses? How do I move forward from weaknesses?	Reach out to others who have gone through a job search. Email Alisha.
	Hide mistakes	Analyze mistakes	What steps do I take to move forward from this mistake?	
	Seek those who praise and avoid critics	Seek critics who give helpful information	Who can give me helpful information? When will I use these resources?	
	Devalue/avoid successful others	Analysis of another's success	What steps have others taken to be successful? Can I take those steps?	

Your chart does not have to be an exact match. But after looking at the example, is there anything you would change or add to your chart for Gerri?

Now let's suppose you are doing the research required to make your next career move. Imagine doing that research. What would it look like? Sometimes that research may be online; sometimes it might involve getting some information from others. Can you visualize the first step? Can you put it in your calendar? What growth mindset obstacles may you encounter as you take that next step? Can you imagine the struggle as you take that next step? Is it possible you may get frustrated or discouraged? Can you do an imagined worst- and best-case scenario for that step using your professional growth mindset chart?

Revising Resume

Now let's suppose, through sustaining a growth mindset, Gerri has researched and identified some promising companies. It has taken a few weeks, but based on what she has read online and people she has spoken to, some companies seem to have more of the team atmosphere she hopes for.

She decides that her next step is to revise and update her resume. She makes a commitment to do this on Saturday and Sunday from 10 to 11 a.m. On Saturday, she pulls up her resume, which she hasn't touched for three years. She reads it, feels good about it, and emails it to a friend to review. On Sunday she gets glowing feedback from her friend, and Gerri says, *Wow. Such a superstar! Let me change a few of the dates, and I'm ready to go.* She changes the dates, and sends the resume out to all the companies she has targeted.

Maybe Gerri's resume is terrific, but can you detect a fixed mindset in her responses? What thoughts, feelings, and reactions might indicate that she has slipped off the growth mindset track? How might these responses get in the way of building and revising her resume and increasing her chances of securing a job she wants?

What patterns are you seeing? Would approaching her resume with more of a growth mindset perspective be valuable to Gerri? What would that look like? What growth mindset coaching might be helpful? Are there some growth mindset actions Gerri might take? What about reaching out to others to review her resume? How about some feedback from some peers who have jobs in a similar industry?

Complete another professional growth mindset chart for Gerri's revision of her resume. Here is an example of how it may be completed. Remember your chart does not have to be a perfect match. Is there anything you would add to your chart after looking at this example?

Gerri's Professional Growth Mindset Chart: Reviewing and Updating Resume

Describe your fixed mindset pothole: *Revising my resume on Saturday and review by a friend*

Circle the type of pothole: (1) facing your challenging task; (2) experience of effort; (3) evaluating progress; (4) making a mistake; (5) praise or criticism; (6) the success or failure of others

FM Thoughts	FM Pattern	GM Pattern	Shift Questions	GM Thoughts
Wow. Such a superstar. Let me change a few of the dates, and I'm ready to go!	All-or-none self-judgment	Analysis of current skill	What is my analysis for improvement? How do I move forward to what I value?	*It feels good that Sheehan thinks my resume is terrific. I wonder what specifically she is responding to? Maybe I can ask if there is anything she might change?*
	-Effort	+Effort	What is a realistic view of the amount of effort required?	*It might take some additional time to revise. I really haven't looked at it for three years.*
	100 percent/ 0 percent performance	Any percent as something	On a continuum, where am I now with progress? What is realistic improvement?	*I wonder how I might tailor it for each of the companies I like?*
	Mistakes as catastrophes	Mistakes as opportunities	What may I learn from my mistake? What can I do differently?	*Also, do I know of anyone else who might give me some input? They may not be as glowing as Sheehan, and yet their edits might be helpful.*
	Others as judges	Others as resources	Are they offering me useful, actionable information?	
	Competitive comparison	Constructive comparison	What may I learn from others? Is there something to be learned from their success?	

FM Emotions	FM Pattern	GM Pattern	Shift Questions	GM Emotions
(mild / ~~moderate~~ / ~~intense~~)	*Good. Proud*		How may I tolerate this? How do I calm myself? *FLOAT*	*Determined. Curious.*

FM Behavior	FM Pattern	GM Pattern	Shift Questions	GM Behavior
Send out after a simple revision of some of the dates	⟨Choose too easy or very difficult tasks⟩	Choose optimal challenges	How do I design a doable, step-by-step growth mindset plan? When will I start?	*Send out to additional folks for input.*
	⟨Decrease/hide effort⟩	Increase efforts	How long will I stay with my plan (despite the effort)?	*Use time allotted on weekends. Assess the strengths and weaknesses and make revisions.*
	Excuses or exaggerations of progress	Accurate assessment of progress	What are my strengths and weaknesses? How do I move forward from weaknesses?	*Reorganize resume to target particular companies.*
	Hide mistakes	Analyze mistakes	What steps do I take to move forward from this mistake?	
	Seek those who praise and avoid critics	Seek critics who give helpful information	Who can give me helpful information? When will I use these resources?	
	Devalue/avoid successful others	Analysis of another's success	What steps have others taken to be successful? Can I take those steps?	

Now let's suppose Gerri had a different reaction to her resume. She pulls it up and says, *This stinks! I don't want anyone to see this! Not good enough! Why bother? Will take too long. My job pays better than most.* She feels embarrassed and discouraged, goes to her kitchen, and eats a bag of potato chips. Then she spends hours on Saturday fussing over details like spacing and the fonts in her resume. Exhausted on Sunday, she avoids working on her resume altogether.

Can you detect a fixed mindset? What are the signals? Use a growth mindset chart to help Gerri with this type of reaction.

After you fill out the chart, look at this example of how it may be completed. Is there anything you would add to Gerri's chart after looking at this example?

Gerri's Professional Growth Mindset Chart: Reviewing and Updating Resume

Describe your fixed mindset pothole: *Revising my resume on Saturday*

Circle the type of pothole: (1) facing your challenging task; (2) experience of effort; (3) evaluating progress; (4) making a mistake;
(5) praise or criticism; (6) the success or failure of others

FM Thoughts	FM Pattern	GM Pattern	Shift Questions	GM Thoughts
This stinks! I don't want anyone to see this! Not good enough!	All-or-none self-judgment	Analysis of current skill	What is my analysis for improvement? How do I move forward to what I value?	*I haven't looked at this for three years, so it's going to take a bit of time. Let me stay with it and stick to my schedule.*
Why bother? Will take too long. My job pays better than most.	-Effort	+Effort	What is a realistic view of the amount of effort required?	*My job does pay well, and yet I'm unhappy with the isolation. This resume is a step to checking out the possibilities.*
	100 percent/ 0 percent performance	Any percent as something	On a continuum, where am I now with progress? What is realistic improvement?	*Are there some folks who could give me some input about my resume? Who do I know in the industry?*
	Mistakes as catastrophes	Mistakes as opportunities	What may I learn from my mistake? What can I do differently?	*I'll make some revisions. It will take some energy and time. It doesn't have to be perfect, just better and up to date. Can I think about making it 25 percent better?*
	Others as judges	Others as resources	Are they offering me useful, actionable information?	*I have skills. I have been working at this job for three years and get great reviews.*
	Competitive comparison	Constructive comparison	What may I learn from others? Is there something to be learned from their success?	*Just have to figure out how to capture my skills in my resume.*

FM Emotions	FM Pattern	GM Pattern	Shift Questions	GM Emotions
(mild/moderate/⟨intense⟩)			How may I tolerate this? How do I calm myself?	
Embarrassed. Discouraged.			Deep breathing. FLOAT	*Calmer, more focused*

FM Behavior	FM Pattern	GM Pattern	Shift Questions	GM Behavior
Eat potato chips. Work obsessively for the next few hours, revising and rewriting and then doing the same again and again.	⟨Choose too easy or very difficult tasks⟩	Choose optimal challenges	How do I design a doable, step-by-step growth mindset plan? When will I start?	*Stay with schedule. Ask some folks to give feedback about strengths and weaknesses of resume.*
Avoid working on resume on Sunday.	Decrease/hide effort	Increase efforts	How long will I stay with my plan (despite the effort)?	*Make more revisions but keep within a schedule and set limits on how long to work on revisions. Set a realistic deadline for finishing.*
	Excuses or exaggerations of progress	Accurate assessment of progress	What are my strengths and weaknesses? How do I move forward from weaknesses?	
	Hide mistakes	Analyze mistakes	What steps do I take to move forward from this mistake?	
	Seek those who praise and avoid critics	Seek critics who give helpful information	Who can give me helpful information? When will I use these resources?	
	Devalue/avoid successful others	Analysis of another's success	What steps have others taken to be successful? Can I take those steps?	

Can you see that Gerri's response to a setback in the second scenario is the flipside of the same coin? Facing the challenging task of revising the resume triggers a fixed mindset in both scenarios that were just described.

How do we know? How can we spot fixed mindset? One clue is the all-or-none evaluation of self. Can you see how the fixed mindset way of judging your ability as "I'm a superstar" or "not good enough" can short-circuit ways of improving your resume? Can you see that although the fixed mindset self-talk and emotions may be different, they both result in disengagement from the task at hand, revising the resume? The superstar Gerri prematurely disengages because she concludes that she has sufficient ability, so there is nothing more to do. The not-good-enough Gerri disengages by avoidance in eating potato chips and through unproductive fussing, losing opportunities for helpful criticism from others or a bigger picture analysis of the strengths and weaknesses of her resume.

Use the growth mindset chart available at http://www.newharbinger.com/48299 to spot the signals of the fixed mindset in yourself and to get on the professional growth mindset path. Employ it to maintain focus and engage with your resume despite distracting thoughts and emotions that pull you away from important growth actions, such as a realistic assessment of your resume and connecting with those who might give you helpful criticism. Imagine revising or creating your resume. Visualize that first step and commit to it despite feeling unsettled. Put it in your calendar.

Networking

You have helped Gerri sustain a growth mindset, and she has revised her resume. Next she tackles networking to increase her chances of finding a job with more of a team environment

Her first step in networking is to post a profile on LinkedIn. She schedules that step on her calendar and completes it quickly, as she has completed her resume.

Her next step is to make a list of potential professional connections. Gerri schedules time in her calendar to read the relevant profiles on LinkedIn and their associated endorsements and testimonials. What growth menaces might lurk there?

Fixed mindset Gerri might say to herself, *Look at how much they have accomplished. I have wasted the last three years. Who will hire me when they have all these others to choose from?* What will she feel given these thoughts? How might this get in the way of taking steps to network?

Alternatively, fixed mindset Gerri might say, *Such lightweights! My profile soars far above theirs.* What will she feel given these thoughts? How might these feelings and thoughts undermine her networking skills? Will she prepare adequately for face-to-face professional connections?

What about you? What would the fixed mindset you think, feel, and do when you read about the accomplishments of others on LinkedIn? What would the growth mindset you think, feel, and do?

Use the growth mindset chart to capture your reactions and signals of potential fixed mindset when you read the posts on LinkedIn. Defend against those reactions with your professional growth mindset responses.

Conducting Informational Interviews

So let's say that you and Gerri have sustained a growth mindset perspective and completed your list of potential professional connections for networking. Next step on the calendar is to prepare for informational interviews with your professional connections. Preparing goes smoothly, as there is a lot on the internet and in books about informational interviewing, including how to introduce yourself, questions to ask (such as "What do you like most and least about the company?"), how to thank people, and how to maintain your connection. Now that the interview prep work is done, what's your next move? Contact, connect, and do an informational interview with those on the list. Easy? Maybe not.

For some people, this step triggers a fixed mindset. If this happens to you, take action to sustain your growth mindset. Informational interviewing and networking are important skills to develop when you wish to make a change in your career. What you learn from talking to people in the industry or visiting them where they work is something that you can't find online.

Some people dodge this action step. They feel uncomfortable and say to themselves, *I'm an introvert* or *just no good at networking,* or they feel smug and tell themselves, *I don't need this step. I'm talented enough to do this on my own.* Or they say, *No need to go through this, I'll just post my resume online.* Can you detect the fixed mindset in these reactions? Is this a professional growth action step that you may dodge because of a fixed mindset? If so, prepare for it. What will your likely thoughts and feelings as you look at your list of contacts? Use the growth mindset chart to anticipate your fixed mindset and sustain your growth mindset.

What else could you do if you dodge this growth action step? How about using a growth hierarchy (introduced in chapter 5) for informational interviews? How would that work here? Complete this hierarchy worksheet.

Hierarchy: Contacts for Informational Interviews

Instructions: Use this worksheet if at times you avoid asking knowledgeable contacts for information that may be helpful to your professional growth.

1. Make a list of professional contacts who may be helpful and rank them in order from easiest to most difficult to approach.

2. Begin with the contact who is least intimidating (row 1) and schedule the date when you will contact them.

3. Contact them and set up a time to meet.

4. Summarize your takeaway from the interview. Write out specific suggestions for growth in your career.

Repeat these steps with the second contact on your list, and so on, until you have conducted all of your interviews.

Rank Order	Date to Contact	Date to Meet	Takeaway from Meeting
1.			
2.			
3.			
4.			

Gerri first practices informational interviewing with family and friends and gets some advice from them about her style and questions. She uses this information to modify her interview. Then she works her way up the hierarchy to contact those leads whom she knows less well, which is more daunting. Here is Gerri's hierarchy of contacts with her takeaways from her first meeting:

Rank Order	Date to Contact	Date to Meet	Takeaway from Meeting
1. Sister	3 p.m. today by email	Next Tuesday at 6 pm	Shorten my introduction. Slow down the questioning. Give them more of a chance to answer.
2. Uncle			
3. Mother's friend			
4. Barry M.			

Say you have created a hierarchy, but you, like others before you, find it hard to make the final—most difficult, most intimidating—contact. What do you do then? What other CBT tools do you have in your pocket? How about a growth coach worksheet (introduced in chapter 3) for professional growth?

First, imagine a worst-case scenario of what an intimidating but important contact will say to you during your informational interview. Perhaps you meet at their place of work, and when you walk into their office, they are not smiling. In fact, they appear annoyed. They look at their watch and out the window as you introduce yourself. You ask questions about their career path and the company, and they grunt a short reply. When, after thirty long minutes, you thank them for their time, they abruptly dismiss you, perhaps saying that you just don't have the experience or education that's needed for work at their company.

Consider your reaction. Be tough. Create in your mind the growth menace, a critical person of authority. Will their sharp words and demeanor trigger a fixed mindset? If so, how would you know? Would you have harsh words about yourself, or would you remain an adoring fan? Some people are more likely to have a harsh critic's responses, whereas others are more likely to respond with the adoring fan, but either response indicates a fixed mindset.

How might you sustain a growth mindset using the helpful strategic coach? What might you say to yourself if this worst-case scenario occurred?

Professional Growth Coach Worksheet

Instructions: Imagine a worst-case scenario interviewer, unsympathetic and fault finding. Would your thoughts about yourself be those of a harsh critic or an adoring fan? Write down your self-talk in column one. In column two, write the growth mindset analysis of the compassionate yet strategic coach.

Harsh Critic/Adoring Fan Self-Talk	Compassionate Yet Strategic Coach

Let's look at Gerri's professional growth coach worksheet. The first one here represents the harsh critic responses when a fixed mindset is triggered by a difficult informational interviewer.

Gerri's Professional Growth Coach Worksheet: Harsh Critic

Harsh Critic/Adoring Fan Self-Talk	Compassionate Yet Strategic Coach
He thinks I don't have what it takes.	It may be that's what he thinks. Perhaps he has a fixed mindset about me, or there is something about my skills he's responding to?
Can't even keep his interest during this interview.	What's important is my takeaway. What useful information have I gained? Certainly from my contact with him, this is not the kind of environment I would enjoy.
How will I ever find a job I enjoy?	He has suggested I don't have the skills and experience. What skills do I have? What skills may I consider growing? How would I grow these skills?
Not worth going through this again.	What experiences do I have that match this company? Are there additional experiences that may be helpful for finding the job I want?
	Not everyone of my interviews will be 100 percent positive and successful. Wonder if there are any other contacts I should consider?

This next chart represents adoring fan self-talk when a challenging informational interview triggers fixed mindset.

Gerri's Professional Growth Coach Worksheet: Adoring Fan

Harsh Critic/Adoring Fan Self-Talk	Compassionate Yet Strategic Coach
What a jerk. He can't see how talented I am! Not worth going through this again, such a waste of time!	It may be that's what he thinks. Perhaps he has a fixed mindset about me, or there is something about my skills he's responding to? What's important is my takeaway. What useful information have I gained? Certainly from my contact with him, this is not the kind of environment I would enjoy. He has suggested I don't have the skills and experience. What skills do I have? What skills may I consider growing? How would I grow those skills? What experiences do I have that match this company? Are there additional experiences that may be helpful for finding the job I want? Not everyone of my interviews will be 100 percent positive and successful. Wonder if there are any other contacts I should consider?

Can you detect a fixed mindset in both harsh critic and adoring fan responses to the challenging informational interview? What are the signals? Can you see what these responses have in common? Facing someone difficult during an informational interview triggers a fixed mindset in both examples. How do we know? How can we spot it? Do you see how both responses short-circuit ways of learning from informational interviews? Can you see that although the fixed mindset self-talk may be different, they both result in disengagement from the task at hand: your takeaways? The superstar Gerri dismisses the critic as a jerk and has no takeaways. The not-good-enough Gerri becomes discouraged and also has no takeaways. Both end up in the same place, avoiding future informational interviews and losing opportunities to learn from others in the industry.

Going to Job Interviews

So you have helped Gerri sustain a growth mindset through all the prep required to apply and interview for jobs. Through the hard work of research, revising a resume, and through her contacts and informational interviewing, she has secured the big job interview in a company that seems to meet her criteria.

Gerri takes the recommended steps to prepare for her interview, anticipating the interviewer's questions about her resume and having answers to questions about her goals and why she has an interest in this company. She has responses to questions about her strengths and weaknesses. She also has come up with questions for the interviewer about the company. She has practiced the interview with friends and learned from their suggestions. In short, she has done her homework incorporating the best practices for interview preparation.

Now comes the mindset part. How does Gerri sustain a growth mindset through the interview process? How does she recognize when a fixed mindset is pulling her off track? It feels like showtime, doesn't it? Gerri has been working hard, practicing, rehearsing. Now it's time for the performance. The interviewer will judge her: thumbs up or thumbs down. Is she talented or not? Everything is on the line. She will either be good enough or not. And it's not just about the job—it's about Gerri and her life!—or is this a fixed mindset way of looking at the interview? How do we know? What thoughts, feelings, and actions would signal Gerri has a fixed mindset approach to the interview? Capture responses that would indicate a fixed mindset on a growth mindset chart, available at http://www.newharbinger.com/48299.

What would be Gerri's responses if she viewed the interview with a growth mindset? Use the prompts in the professional growth mindset chart to sustain a growth mindset for the job interview. Can you make the shift to a growth mindset?

Of course, the above example is just one type of fixed mindset response to an interview. There are others. What if instead of feeling nervous about the interview, Gerri felt a bit smug and said to herself, *I've got this nailed*? How would this mindset impact her preparation for the interview? How would this mindset affect her if during the interview she stumbles over a questions? What if she thought she would nail it and then was not offered the job? How might it impact her ability to rebound from such a rejection?

Now it's your turn: imagine an interview for a job that is incredibly significant to you. Put yourself in that moment. Imagine the day of the interview. You arrive early and wait. You're greeted, and you walk through the door and sit down in front of the interviewer. What are your feelings as you walk through the door. What are your thoughts? Do you detect any fixed mindset thoughts or feelings? If so, what would they be? Capture them on another professional growth mindset chart.

Maybe you have such thoughts and feelings about interviews, or maybe you don't. If you do, it's not unusual. Many people have such responses. Interviews are challenging. They're not easy, and that's okay: it takes some effort to prepare and sustain a growth mindset. What's important is that now you have a chance to inoculate yourself against the fixed mindset by shoring up your growth mindset responses to this challenge.

Summary

Without awareness, fixed mindset can sidetrack your professional growth: entangle you in career-limiting thinking, distract you with unhelpful emotions, and narrow and restrict your occupational options. Apply lessons learned about the growth mindset to get back on the road toward a more fulfilling work life.

- Unpack your professional dissatisfaction and turn it into a professional growth goal.

- Visualize a step toward that professional goal and commit to it.

- Detect and defend against six growth mindset menaces that hamper professional progress with the Growth Mindset Chart and other CBT tools.

With this plan, you'll construct your growth mindset platform to escape from the fixed mindset: coaching yourself with career enhancing self-talk, climbing upward toward your professional goal, letting go of limiting emotions, and taking steps forward despite the urge to stay where you are in your current job because it feels safe.

CHAPTER 8

A Growth Mindset for Everyday Life

In the chapter 7, you learned to apply the growth mindset for a large change in your life: to develop your career. Now let's make the growth mindset something you can use every day. How might you use it to enrich and expand your daily life and tackle everyday challenges? How do you apply the growth mindset to improve relationships, your health, or your emotional well-being? This chapter is an opportunity to consider the possibilities.

If you find that most of your days are energized by a growth mindset, no need to read further. However, you may discover that a fixed mindset traps you into a daily routine that feels predictable and safe but is dissatisfying. Let's follow Doran as he grapples with dissatisfaction in his daily life. Doran is divorced and lives alone in an apartment. He likes his job as an auto mechanic but has fallen into a routine after work that bothers him. His days are long, so he usually gets takeout at the local deli, has a couple of beers, watches some sports on cable TV, and falls asleep. Then he repeats the same the next weekday and the next. What he does after work has been his pattern for the last couple of years since his divorce. He has put on some weight and feels lethargic. Weekends, he hangs with some high school friends at the local bar. He feels bored, restless, and lonely. Can you see the signals of fixed mindset in Doran's daily life?

Personal dissatisfactions don't have to be big to weigh you down every day. They gnaw at you. They pester you. For example, some people are bothered because they lack a meaningful connection with their children or their partners; others by a sense that they can't get a handle on their day-to-day finances. Others are distressed by their daily habits. Others are concerned they are not using their spare time in productive, relaxing, or healthy ways.

It may not even occur to you that you could change these aggravations with a growth mindset and live a daily life aligned with your values. This chapter will show you how to:

- Unpack an everyday dissatisfaction and turn it into a personal growth goal

- Use a personal growth goal worksheet to organize your growth action plan

- Employ your growth mindset defenses daily to maintain your progress

Continue reading if you are dissatisfied with your usual routines and would like to apply growth mindset skills to expand and enrich your everyday life.

Turn Your Dissatisfaction into a Personal Growth Goal

A fixed mindset can confine you in a daily routine that feels predictable and safe but is dissatisfying. Could this be you? Would your life be more fulfilling if you defined some personal growth goals?

Define Your Personal Growth Goals

Part 1. Identify specific areas of dissatisfaction in your daily life by responding to the following questions.

1. Is it something about what you do in your downtime, in the evening or on weekends? Have you fallen into a rut that is predictable but dissatisfying or boring? For example, streaming a series, gaming, or following others on social media and then falling into bed?

   _____

2. Do you have downtime or free time? Are you dissatisfied with your emotional well-being? Are you feeling overwhelmed or stressed?

   _____

3. Is it something about your physical well-being? Do you think you should get more exercise or eat more healthfully but, after attempts to do so, find yourself back in old habits—engaging in sedentary activities, getting little exercise, and eating food that's not very good for you?

   _____

4. Is it something about your relationships? Do you feel isolated or lonely? Or, maybe you have many daily interactions but find few that are satisfying? What about your close relationships with partners, children, and parents? Do you feel unconnected? Are your current relationships stressful? Do you feel unsupported or unappreciated?

   _____

5. Are there any ways that you are dissatisfied in your everyday life? Remember, these dissatisfactions don't have to be big, but they weigh you down every day.

   _____

Write your specific dissatisfactions in your everyday life here:

_____

_____

_____

Part 2. Turn this dissatisfaction into an everyday personal goal by responding to the following questions:

1. Is there an activity today that you think may be interesting, but you have avoided out of concern for failing or looking foolish?

    _____

2. Is there something you could do today, that you value, but you've avoided it and avoided stretching yourself because you don't want to find out that you're not good at it?

    _____

3. Are there activities during your day that feel safe but boring? These may be ones where you feel confident that you can show yourself to be competent (or even talented), but perhaps you find that you're a bit weary of them? What daily activities or activity today may be more fun or interesting but feel a bit risky?

    _____

4. Are there some activities today that you would like to try, but are concerned that you lack the ability?

    _____

5. Are there daily changes that you've tried to make but became frustrated and then gave up? Would you value these changes if you felt you could make them with little effort?

    _____

6. Were there times in your everyday life when you felt challenged and excited about learning something new? What was that activity? Can you still feel that excitement? Can you feel that excitement, along with some natural trepidations, as you contemplate something new? What were the aspects of that activity that you enjoyed? Is there a similar activity now that you may engage in today or daily?

    _____

Based on your responses, can you think of an everyday growth goal that may excite you, even though when you consider it, you get scared, feel avoidant, and perhaps, fear failing? A goal where stretching yourself would increase your satisfaction?

Write out your personal growth goal here:

_____

_____

_____

Coming up with a personal growth goal is not easy, especially if you have been caught up in a daily fixed mindset. The fixed mindset confines you, and you dwell there without awareness. Everything seems all right. But is it? Is this the daily life that aligns with what you value?

Give yourself time to grapple with the possibilities. You may need a series of appointments with yourself. Your options for everyday growth don't have to be perfect or big, just a step closer to a life that is meaningful to you. Sometimes you don't know until you run an experiment and stick with it for a while. So for example, I worked with someone who took a class in jewelry making even though she didn't think she had the talent for it. It became a significant part of her life; she loved the creative process and made some new friends as she took classes.

If you are bored or dissatisfied with your daily life, how would you challenge yourself if you weren't concerned with failing? Would you take an online course? Learn to play a musical instrument? It doesn't have to be a piano or something big. How about a ukulele or a harmonica?

How about going to night school? Look at the offerings: anything in the catalogs catch your eye? How about learn a new language or return to learning a language you abandoned? Learn to play a new sport or return to an old sport?

If you weren't concerned with playing it safe, would you make new friends? Try a new hobby?

If you weren't concerned with looking bad, would you learn to dance or sing? Take a meditation class, see a therapist or marriage counselor?

If you thought you could do so with little effort, would you spend more time with friends, reconnect with your family? Develop your spiritual self or return to a place of worship or explore a new place of worship? Volunteer in your community? Renovate your home? Take up gardening? What are the possibilities?

Let's track how Doran defines his personal growth goals with this worksheet. First he makes a series of fifteen-minute appointments with himself to ponder the part 1 and part 2 questions about his daily life. He designates fifteen minutes after dinner on Monday, Tuesday, and Wednesday and marks his calendar.

First Doran tackles part 1, identifying specific areas of dissatisfaction in his daily life. He responds to the questions that he finds most relevant:

- Is it something about what you do in your downtime, in the evening or on the weekends? Have you fallen into a rut that is predictable but dissatisfying or boring?

  Same routine every weeknight, dinner and then cable TV sports and then fall asleep.

- Do you have downtime or free time? Are you dissatisfied with your emotional well-being? Are you feeling overwhelmed or stressed?

  Not stressed, just bored and restless.

- Is it something about your physical well-being? Do you think you should get more exercise or eat more healthfully but, after attempts to do so, find yourself back in old habits—engaging in sedentary activities, getting little exercise, and eating food that's not very good for you?

  Eat too many hoagies, drink too much beer, not exercising. Diabetes runs in family.

- Is it something about your relationships? Do you feel isolated or lonely? Or, maybe you have many daily interactions but find few that are satisfying? What about your close relationships with partners, children, and parents? Do you feel unconnected? Are your current relationships stressful? Do you feel unsupported or unappreciated?

  Like guys at work but lonely during weeknights.

- Are there any other ways that you are dissatisfied in your everyday life? Remember, these dissatisfactions don't have to be big, but they weigh you down every day.

For specific dissatisfactions at the end of this list, Doran writes:

1. *Diet of hoagies and beer and no exercise will lead to diabetes that runs in my family.*

2. *Bored, restless, and lonely; feel there must be something more outside my job.*

Then under part 2, Doran turns his dissatisfaction into an everyday personal goal. Again he respond to the questions that he finds most relevant:

- Is there a daily activity or activity today that you think may be interesting, but you have avoided out of concern for failing or looking foolish?

  Whittling! Who whittles? Not a manly thing.

- Are there activities during your day that feel safe but boring? What daily activities or activity today may be more fun or interesting but feel a bit risky?

  Bored! Thought about the local Y, lifting weights. Might be fun but really don't know anyone who goes to the Y, and I'm beyond out-of-shape.

- Are there some activities today that you would try, activities that you would like to try, but are concerned that you lack the ability?

  Pickup basketball at the Y, haven't played since high school. Will really suck at it.

- Are there daily changes that you've tried to make but became frustrated and then gave up? Would you value these changes if you felt you could make them with little effort?

  Eat something different at dinner, drink less beer but tired after work—not worth the effort. Tried to mix it up by making salads and having just one beer, but could only do it for a couple of weeks.

- Were there times in your everyday life when you felt challenged and excited about learning something new? What was that activity? Can you still feel that excitement? Can you feel that excitement, along with some natural trepidations, as you contemplate something new? What were the aspects of that activity that you enjoyed? Is there a similar activity now that you may engage in today or daily?

  Excited when I learned to be a mechanic. Awesome feeling when I've figured out what's wrong with a car and then fix it. Like to work with my hands. Whittling. Learned it from my uncle, who was a pro. Made a few carvings, mainly fish. It was fun and relaxing. Could still do it. All it requires is a knife and some soft wood.

In short, Doran turns his dissatisfaction into a growth goal, asking himself, *What would my time after work look like if I weren't concerned about failing, playing it safe, or looking bad? What would I do if I could do it with little effort?*

For his personal growth goals, Doran writes: *Learn to make healthier foods, improve fitness, and develop new relationships through pickup basketball. Improve skills at whittling in spare time.*

Use a Growth Goal Worksheet to Organize an Action Plan

Now that you have a personal growth goal, let's use the growth goal worksheet from chapter 2 to organize your plan for your everyday goals. Download a copy of the growth goal worksheet at http://www.newharbinger.com/48299 and fill it out to organize an action plan.

Let's illustrate how to do this with Doran's responses to the growth goal worksheet. He has three personal growth goals:

1. Personal growth goal: *Learn to make some healthier foods.*

   First small step (visualize): *Shop on Wednesday night and buy some healthy options; experiment with recipes.*

   Even-though feeling: *It will be too much effort after working all day.*

   Schedule step on calendar: *Next Wednesday*

2. Personal growth goal: *Improve fitness and meet others through pickup basketball at the Y.*

   First small step (visualize): *Go to Y Tuesday and Thursday for pickup games.*

   Even-though feeling: *Out of shape and don't know anyone*

   Schedule step on calendar: *Next Tuesday and Thursday*

3. Personal growth goal: *Improve whittling skills in spare time*

   First Step (visualize) *Get knife and sticks out of closet and start.*

   Even-though feeling: *Seems silly*

   Schedule step on calendar: *Next Monday after dinner*

Now it's your turn to complete your own personal growth goal worksheet.

Employ Your Growth Mindset Defenses Daily

After you complete your personal growth goal worksheet, what happens next? Do you just adopt a growth mindset? Wave your magic growth mindset wand and, presto, all your daily dissatisfactions disappear? That would be amazing! Having understood the advantages of the growth mindset, you simply wave the growth mindset wand—living every day and in every way in growth mindedness.

If we were to wave the growth mindset wand for Doran, what might we imagine about his daily life in a constant state of growth mindedness? How about Doran creates a food blog where he makes gourmet healthy meals that save the planet? He is so talented at pickup basketball that everyone wants to play with him and be his buddy. He has found a passion for whittling, has posted his projects on YouTube, and has hundreds of followers. But is this really a growth mindset or an entrapment in a fixed mindset—a Facebook fantasy life about the growth mindset? Is it realistic to think that now Doran understands the growth mindset and does his worksheets, he is living a life he values?

What do we know about the reality of adopting a growth mindset? It is not always easy, but that's okay. Just because it is hard doesn't mean you can't move toward a daily life that you value. Embrace the struggle and take that first small step and then the next. Effort is expected when you are trying to develop. It's about daily small steps and warding off the growth menaces.

Let's look at the real Doran, who would like to make some meaningful changes in his life but, like many others, sometimes struggles to maintain a growth mindset. Doran had to ward off a number of growth menaces as he took his daily growth steps.

He has joined the Y and is playing pickup basketball. He gets winded and isn't the best player on the court, but he sees he's developing more stamina and getting better with practice. Although initially hesitant, awkward, and uncomfortable, he has made an effort to introduce himself at the Y and asks all of the regular players to join him for a quick dinner out. Some people said yes, and others said maybe next time. Overall, this has led to a couple of new friendships. One of his friends has included him for casual friend and family cookouts, perhaps the beginning of some enduring relationships. He has been asking others about their favorite dishes. Although it takes some effort to shop for the ingredients and prepare, he's experimenting with store-bought pizza crust and adding new heathier toppings like arugula and eggplant, and he has invited a couple of neighbors over for pizza night. He's found that although he doesn't like arugula, he likes eggplant and enjoys some variety in his diet. Next, he visualizes making some more interesting salads. How about making his own dressing?

He has started whittling again, and although initially frustrated with his progress, he has stuck with it. He finds it relaxing and gets satisfaction in transforming pieces of wood into detailed small animals. After a long hiatus, he has reached out to his uncle who taught him how to whittle. He has begun to rekindle a connection with a family member whom he realizes he missed.

Doran has turned his dissatisfaction with his daily life into some personal growth goals and visualized and committed to taking some specific steps. Some of these steps were easy for Doran, and other steps were more difficult.

This is not the Facebook fantasy outcome for Doran's daily life. It is the any-percent-is something version and much improved over his previous life. Consider Doran's fixed mindset challenges as he has tried to grow in his everyday life. For example, with pickup basketball, Doran is out-of-shape and winded and not the best on the court. If this were magical growth mindset time, this would not bother him, and he would play basketball with little discomfort or unease. The reality for Doran, however, is that he sometimes falls into a fixed mindset about his basketball abilities. He has to pause and spot the red flags in this thoughts (*I'm such a dork. Shouldn't feel this tired after twenty minutes. Everyone else is looking good*), in his feelings (discouraged and embarrassed), and in his actions (cut out early, make excuses, avoid the next game, negate others).

Download a growth mindset chart at http://www.newharbinger.com/48299 to help Doran capture the signals of a fixed mindset. Can you help him shift back to a growth mindset by completing the chart for him?

Afterward, look at this example of Doran's completed chart and possible growth mindset responses. Is there anything you would add to or change about your chart for Doran?

Doran's Personal Growth Mindset Chart: Basketball

Describe your fixed mindset pothole: *Winded after twenty minutes, other players not sweating*

Circle the type of pothole: (1) facing your challenging task; (2) experience of effort; (3) evaluating progress; (4) making a mistake; (5) praise or criticism; (6) the success or failure of others

FM Thoughts	FM Pattern	GM Pattern	Shift Questions	GM Thoughts
I'm such a dork. Shouldn't feel this tired after twenty minutes.	All-or-none self-judgment	Analysis of current skill	What is my analysis for improvement? How do I move forward to what I value?	I haven't played since high school. It will take a while to get back in shape. At least I have begun, and I like being back in the game.
Everyone else is looking good.	-Effort	+Effort	What is a realistic view of the amount of effort required?	My stamina is not great at this point, but my shots are not bad.
	100 percent/ 0 percent performance	Any percent as something	On a continuum, where am I now with progress? What is realistic improvement?	Wonder if there is something else I might do to increase my aerobic fitness?
	Mistakes as catastrophes	Mistakes as opportunities	What may I learn from my mistake? What can I do differently?	I'm not competing for a spot on the Lakers. I'm here to have fun and get some exercise.
	Others as judges	Others as resources	Are they offering me useful, actionable information?	I could ask others how long and how often they play, and what else they do to keep fit.
	Competitive comparison	Constructive comparison	What may I learn from others? Is there something to be learned from their success?	

FM Emotions	FM Pattern	GM Pattern	Shift Questions	GM Emotions
(mild / moderate / intense)			How may I tolerate this? How do I calm myself?	
Embarrassed, discouraged			Here-and-now focusing. FLOAT.	More at ease, relaxed

FM Behavior	FM Pattern	GM Pattern	Shift Questions	GM Behavior
Cut out early.	Choose too easy or very difficult tasks	Choose optimal challenges	How do I design a doable, step-by-step growth mindset plan? When will I start?	Stay in the game despite fatigue.
Let others know I have a knee problem from an old football injury.	Decrease/hide effort	Increase efforts	How long will I stay with my plan (despite the effort)?	Fess up to others that I'm a bit out of shape, so it might take more games to build stamina.
Avoid next pickup game.	Excuses or exaggerations of progress	Accurate assessment of progress	What are my strengths and weaknesses? How do I move forward from weaknesses?	Stick with plan to participate in pickup basketball regularly.
Tell self that they are a bunch of losers with nothing better to do with their lives.	Hide mistakes	Analyze mistakes	What steps do I take to move forward from this mistake?	Use suggestions of others, like do some jogging on weekends to increase aerobic fitness.
	Seek those who praise and avoid critics	Seek critics who give helpful information	Who can give me helpful information? When will I use these resources?	
	Devalue/avoid successful others	Analysis of another's success	What steps have others taken to be successful? Can I take those steps?	

Now consider Doran's challenges as he has attempted concrete steps to develop everyday relationships. After going to the gym for a few weeks, he commits to the step of asking all the regulars at basketball to join him for a quick dinner. Two people say yes and the rest say no.

It would be nice if we could simply wave the growth mindset wand, and this response to his invitation wouldn't upset Doran. He would simply go to dinner with the two people who said yes and be on his way to developing everyday relationships. But is this what happens? In reality, Doran feels irritated and discouraged. He thinks, *Not cool enough to get everyone to join me. They think I'm a dork. Not worth putting myself out there.* Can you see that the shift in Doran's emotions is connected to a fixed mindset pothole? What is the pothole? Do you see the signs of a fixed mindset in his thoughts? If Doran doesn't identify it and shift to a growth mindset, what impact might this have on everyday action steps to develop more friendships? Will he avoid and criticize the others who declined his invitation? Will he persist in initiating activities with others?

Capture Doran's reactions to people declining his invitation in another personal growth mindset chart. Can you use the chart to help Doran shift back to his growth action plan to improve his everyday relationships? After completing Doran's chart, look at this example of a complete chart. Is there anything you would add to your chart for Doran?

Doran's Personal Growth Mindset Chart: Extend Self to Others

Describe your fixed mindset pothole: *Two people join me for dinner, and the rest say no.*

Circle the type of pothole: (1) facing your challenging task; (2) experience of effort; (3) evaluating progress; (4) making a mistake; (5) praise or criticism; (6) the success or failure of others

FM Thoughts	FM Pattern	GM Pattern	Shift Questions	GM Thoughts
Not cool enough to get everyone to join me.	(All-or-none self-judgment)	Analysis of current skill	What is my analysis for improvement? How do I move forward to what I value?	My goal was to ask others to dinner. I did that.
They think I'm a dork.				Is it realistic to think that with just one invitation, everyone will say yes and I will have instant friendships? It takes a while to get to know others, and friendships require some time.
Not worth putting myself out there.	(-Effort)	+Effort	What is a realistic view of the amount of effort required?	
	(100 percent/ 0 percent performance)	Any percent as something	On a continuum, where am I now with progress? What is realistic improvement?	Maybe dinner is too big of a commitment. Next time I'll ask others to join me for a quick drink. Allow that some may already have friends and family commitments.
	Mistakes as catastrophes	Mistakes as opportunities	What may I learn from my mistake? What can I do differently?	Could be, they think I'm a dork. I may never know, but it's about connecting with some people I might enjoy. Not sure at this point who that will be. Only way to find out is to continue to put myself out to others.
	(Others as judges)	Others as resources	Are they offering me useful, actionable information?	
	Competitive comparison	Constructive comparison	What may I learn from others? Is there something to be learned from their success?	How about a hierarchy? Instead of asking everyone to join me, maybe I start with someone easy to approach and then move on to someone a bit less approachable

FM Emotions	FM Pattern	GM Pattern	Shift Questions	GM Emotions
(mild/moderate/intense) *Irritated, discouraged*			How may I tolerate this? How do I calm myself? *Deep Breathing. FLOAT*	*Sad, but determined*

FM Behavior	FM Pattern	GM Pattern	Shift Questions	GM Behavior
Avoid those who said no to invitation.	Choose too easy or very difficult tasks	Choose optimal challenges	How do I design a doable, step-by-step growth mindset plan? When will I start?	*Create a hierarchy with people of interest, from easiest to most difficult to approach.*
Tell those who join me for dinner that the others are full of themselves.	Decrease/hide effort	Increase efforts	How long will I stay with my plan (despite the effort)?	*Ask them out for coffee or drinks again after pickup game. Do this two more times.*
Give up asking others out. Wait until they approach me.	Excuses or exaggerations of progress	Accurate assessment of progress	What are my strengths and weaknesses? How do I move forward from weaknesses?	*See if they reciprocate. If not, put my energy with the two people who have joined me.*
	Hide mistakes	Analyze mistakes	What steps do I take to move forward from this mistake?	*Explore other ways of meeting new people— weight-lifting class at gym; throw cookout for a few neighbors in apartment complex.*
	Seek those who praise and avoid critics	Seek critics who give helpful information	Who can give me helpful information? When will I use these resources?	
	Devalue/avoid successful others	Analysis of another's success	What steps have others taken to be successful? Can I take those steps?	

How about whittling? What growth menaces might Doran encounter daily as he tries to get back into this hobby that once brought him pleasure? What about connecting with his whittling teacher uncle after a long hiatus? The Facebook fantasy is that he develops a following of hundreds on YouTube. The reality is that he decides to whittle a bird dog. It is hard to get back his skills with the knife. He hasn't tried this for over a decade. He makes many attempts and discards many sticks of partially formed bird dogs. He uses the FLOAT technique to deal with his frustration. Eventually, he makes whittling a part of a nighttime routine. He immerses himself in it for about thirty minutes each night and is delighted that some of his skills seem to be coming back to him, as his latest version of a bird dog begins to take shape. He whittles and listens to his favorite bluegrass music, and feels calm, relaxed, and focused. Then, one weekend, his uncle, the pro whittler, visits, sees Doran's latest bird dog, and casually comments, "Nice cat."

What is the growth menace that Doran has encountered as he tries to improve his whittling skills? What reactions to his uncle's cat comment would signal a fixed mindset? Play with Doran's possible reactions. Write down the thoughts, feelings, and actions that would indicate a fixed mindset in a personal growth mindset chart. Then, use the chart to turn his fixed mindset responses around and build a growth mindset.

After you define your personal growth goal and commit to specific steps toward it, be prepared for the possibility that you may fall into a fixed mindset trap—it's to be expected. Is there anyone who never falls into a fixed mindset in any aspect of their lives? Maybe. Maybe babies.

Have you ever watched a baby learn to walk—take those first steps? First, they grab the edge of the coffee table or sofa and cruise along it. They may take a caretaker's hand for support and balance as they practice. Eventually they let go, take a few steps and fall. They trip or lose their balance, push back up, and then take more steps. Think of a baby as she moves from crawling to walking. Growing skills and expanding her universe. Walking is a challenge that babies face daily. What growth menaces do they encounter? Consider them—facing something they haven't done before, seeing others walk when they can't, falling on their face, experiencing the struggle, watching others laugh when they fall.

Let's play with this. Imagine a baby with highly developed cognitive and emotional skills: superbaby. That is, she has adult language and talks to baby friends but can't walk yet. What if the baby fell into a fixed mindset? What would a fixed mindset about walking be? *Do I have what it takes to be a walker? Am I a walker or not?* How would the baby respond to the growth menaces with a fixed mindset? Look at the growth mindset chart and the list of possible fixed mindset potholes.

For example, the baby sees the success of those around them: walking better and walking a lot with little difficulty. What baby thoughts, feelings, and actions indicate a fixed mindset? Use a growth mindset chart to capture the red flags of a fixed mindset. Then use the chart to help this baby maintain a growth mindset.

Here is an example of the walking baby's growth mindset chart. Anything you would add to the baby's chart after looking at this?

Baby's Growth Mindset Chart

Describe your fixed mindset pothole: *Learning to walk*

Circle the type of pothole: (1) facing your challenging task; (2) experience of effort; (3) evaluating progress; (4) making a mistake; (5) praise or criticism; (6) the success or failure of others

Circle the type of pothole: ((1) facing your challenging task) ((2) experience of effort) ((3) evaluating progress) ((4) making a mistake)
((5) praise or criticism) ((6) the success or failure of others)

FM Thoughts	FM Pattern	GM Pattern	Shift Questions	GM Thoughts
I'm not a walker. I don't have what it takes to be a walker. I just fell, which means I'll never walk.	(All-or-none self-judgment)	Analysis of current skill	What is my analysis for improvement? How do I move forward to what I value?	Not many thoughts, intently focused on task at hand. Let's go for it—let go of table—see what happens. Oops, too soon. Let me practice cruising for a while and see what happens.
My goal is to walk a mile on my own today. If I can't. I don't have what it takes!	(-Effort)	+Effort	What is a realistic view of the amount of effort required?	Others are walking. How are they doing that? Don't seem to be walking as quickly, bending their knees, not walking with such straight, stiff legs.
I only walked two steps today. That means I'm not a walker! Why bother?	(100 percent/ 0 percent performance)	Any percent as something	On a continuum, where am I now with progress? What is realistic improvement?	Can I get some help with this? Maybe grab my older brother's hand until I gain more balance?
Others can walk really well. They can walk without falling so easily. They walk for miles, but I can't.	(Mistakes as catastrophes)	Mistakes as opportunities	What may I learn from my mistake? What can I do differently?	Learning to walk is not easy, but I'll stick with it a bit each day. Take a break to eat and play.
I should be able to walk like them. I fell and people laughed. It means I can't do this.	(Others as judges) (Competitive comparison)	Others as resources / Constructive comparison	Are they offering me useful, actionable information? What may I learn from others? Is there something to be learned from their success?	I let go twice and took two steps. Before I was only crawling and cruising!

FM Emotions	FM Pattern	GM Pattern	Shift Questions	GM Emotions
(mild/moderate/intense)			How may I tolerate this? How do I calm myself?	Focused, optimistic, engaged
Frustrated, discouraged, anxious			Deep breathing. Here-and-now focusing. FLOAT.	

FM Behavior	FM Pattern	GM Pattern	Shift Questions	GM Behavior
Stick with crawling. Don't let go of caretaker's hand.	Choose too easy or very difficult tasks	Choose optimal challenges	How do I design a doable, step-by-step growth mindset plan? When will I start?	Start with crawling. Move to cruising.
Try to walk a mile.	Decrease/hide effort	Increase efforts	How long will I stay with my plan (despite the effort)?	Practice daily when not sleeping or eating or playing.
Only practice walking alone, so no one sees me fall, mess up.	Excuses or exaggerations of progress	Accurate assessment of progress	What are my strengths and weaknesses? How do I move forward from weaknesses?	When I fall, get up, practice some more.
Say to younger baby friends, walking is overrated.	Hide mistakes	Analyze mistakes	What steps do I take to move forward from this mistake?	Walk a bit more cautiously, bend knees more, arms out for balance.
Hang with baby friends who don't walk. Avoid hanging with those who can.	Seek those who praise and avoid critics	Seek critics who give helpful information	Who can give me helpful information? When will I use these resources?	Watch caretakers and brother, who have been walking for a long time. Take clues. Model what they do. Walk differently and not as fast.
Say to baby friends, I could walk a mile if I wanted to, but I've got better things to do.	Devalue/avoid successful others	Analysis of another's success	What steps have others taken to be successful? Can I take those steps?	

What's the point of this exercise? I don't know any superbabies with the cognitive capacity of adults, but can you imagine how all this fixed mindset static would hamper a baby's daily growth steps? What if babies were concerned with looking foolish, making mistakes, playing it safe—would they put in all that effort to learn? Would they be persistent? Thank goodness that babies don't have this fixed mindset static; they might spend a lifetime crawling. Most of us, however, do experience fixed mindset static. For some of us, it is loud when we're trying to grow in certain areas and not so loud in other areas. For some of us it is louder than it is for others. For some of us, it is deafening. Even if you don't understand how or when you acquired your fixed mindset, you can learn to turn down the volume and move toward a daily life you value.

What are your potential daily fixed mindset obstacles as you move forward? Look at your personal growth goal worksheets and the concrete steps you've taken or plan to take toward your goal. Some of the steps may be a piece of cake. With other steps, you may be tripped up by a fixed mindset. You can create imagined worst- and best-case scenario personal growth mindset charts with these riskier steps to inoculate and defend against fixed mindset potholes and to practice building your growth mindset scaffolding.

Some people feel that all of the above seems like a lot of work to change your daily life. They ask, "How can I make the time to do all this? I can't do all these charts and worksheets the rest of my life!"

Change is hard. But don't mistake the hardness for impossibility. Don't let the difficulty get in your way. What happens is that with practice and time you will integrate awareness of the fixed mindset and your defense strategies into your daily routine. They become a new habit.

Eventually, you will need to use all the charts and worksheets only on occasions when you discover you are deeply mired in a fixed mindset. If you have ever learned to drive, you may recall the first time you sat in the driver's seat and all the focused concentration required to press the pedals, stay between the lines, and turn the wheel. With time, it became an effortless habit, except on that occasion when you hit a pothole or ice patch and had to mindfully drive the car to deal with the consequences.

When you have integrated these lessons into your daily routine, you can make a brief weekly appointment with yourself to reflect on your progress. Consider doing a week-in-review of your personal growth goals. Reflect on the past week and your personal growth goals: Did you encounter setbacks, such as mistakes or criticism? Did you respond in a growth or fixed mindset way? How do you know? What were the indicators in terms of thoughts, feelings, and actions? What were the patterns in your thinking, such as "any percent is something" versus "100 percent or nothing"? What about your emotions when you encountered these potholes—was there a shift in how you felt? What about your behavior—was it marked by avoidance or by engagement?

If you find that you were mostly in a growth mindset during the week, wonderful. Undertaking the above analysis will strengthen your growth mindset. If you found yourself mainly in a fixed mindset, also wonderful! This gives you an opportunity to regain your growth mindset through the techniques that have been described. For example, take fifteen minutes to:

1. Practice growth mindset charting. Fill out the chart for one of the times you stumbled into a fixed mindset and use the prompts to shift to a growth mindset.

2. Respond to harsh critic/adoring fan self-talk with a growth coach worksheet.

3. Practice calming your fixed mindset emotions with a technique of your choice, such as FLOAT or diaphragmatic breathing.

4. Practice by devising a doable growth action plan despite your apprehension.

5. Reread parts of this book to refresh your memory.

A fifteen-minute investment in any one of these techniques brings you closer to living a daily life aligned with your values.

Summary

A fixed mindset can trap you into a daily routine that feels predictable and safe but is dissatisfying. Apply lessons learned about the growth mindset to enrich and expand your daily life and tackle everyday challenges.

- Unpack your everyday dissatisfaction and turn it into a personal growth goal.

- Visualize a step toward that personal goal and commit to it.

- Detect and defend against the six growth mindset menaces that trap you in a dissatisfying daily routine with the growth mindset chart and other CBT tools.

Employ your growth mindset defenses daily, and set up a weekly appointment with yourself to review your progress toward your goals.

Conclusion: How to Keep a Growth Mindset When the Going Gets Tough

This workbook has built upon Dweck's book *Mindset* and serves as your road map for keeping a growth mindset as you deal with life's expected obstacles. The fixed mindset is the belief that you have a certain amount of an ability or attribute—perhaps high, perhaps low—and that there is little that you can do to change this. The growth mindset is the belief that although you may start with a particular level of ability or attribute, you can increase your ability or develop your attribute.

When people are in a growth mindset, they take on more challenges, they are more resilient in the face of difficulty (adapting and learning from mistakes), and they use other people as mentors or resources to develop their abilities or attributes. In the fixed mindset, people are always worried about their fixed abilities and attributes. Am I smart? Am I talented? Am I likable? Am I weak? Am I a loser? They arrange their worlds to avoid any unwanted answers to these questions. So they choose safe or easy tasks, they run from setbacks, and avoid asking for help from others lest they seem to have deficiencies.

Some people typically have a growth mindset while others typically have a fixed mindset. However, even those who usually have a growth mindset may become mired in a fixed mindset when they hit one of life's potholes (such as setbacks, criticism, mistakes, the success of others). The good news is that there are tools rooted in CBT that can put you back on track. In this book you have been shown how to use these tools to recognize the fixed mindset and thrive through the challenges of life in order to excel in areas of importance to you, be they achievement, social, or personal.

Now it is your turn to strengthen and sustain your growth mindset. Cultivating a growth mindset is much like cultivating a garden. It is not about being a good gardener or a bad gardener. It is about developing gardening skills in the face of many challenges. It is not about simply dropping a seed into the ground and hoping for the best. It takes effort and persistence in the face of obstacles. For instance, what plants do you wish to cultivate? What is the soil like? Is the soil problematic, too rocky or too sandy? Are there insects and pests? How do you control them without harming beneficial insects? Is there not enough or too much rain? You have the seeds for your garden: your growth goals. Consider this book a small starter pot with some tools to cultivate them.

Accept that changing from a fixed mindset to a growth mindset is a process and takes time and continual effort. Just because you have a valued growth goal and understand the difference between a fixed and growth mindset does not mean the pursuit of that goal will happen in a continuous unremitting state of growth mindedness. Try not to fall into the trap of having a fixed mindset about a growth mindset. It is not about *Now I'm a growth mindset person.* The process involves decreasing the frequency, intensity, and duration of fixed mindset thoughts, behaviors, and emotions and increasing the frequency, intensity, and duration of growth mindset thoughts, behaviors, and emotions. It involves getting better at recognizing when you have stumbled into a fixed mindset pothole and then using your CBT skills to build a growth mindset scaffolding to climb out of it and resume your journey to a life you value.

This process is not about the complete elimination of fixed mindsets. Fixed mindsets are a part of the landscape. Fixed mindsets happen! You, as an imperfect, developing human being, will have fixed mindset thoughts, emotions, and behaviors. Your descent into the fixed mindset is an opportunity to become more skilled at building your growth mindset scaffolding.

Expect that a fixed mindset will catch you unaware. A fixed mindset perspective can be so pervasive and automatic that you may not recognize it until after some time has passed. For example, looking back, you may say, "I can't believe I responded to that suggestion from my boss with a fixed mindset," or "I used a competitive comparison and had denigrating thoughts about my friend when she just got a great new job offer." That is okay. Even when it takes you years to recognize that you had been ensnared in a fixed mindset, it is never too late to use the techniques in the book and reframe and learn from the experience using your growth mindset practices. Doing so will make you more resilient and help you navigate back toward a life that is more fulfilling to you.

Just remember that any percent is something. Each time you spot a fixed mindset, even after the fact, it is a step toward developing your growth mindset skills. It takes effort to develop these skills, and you will slip up and make mistakes. You are well on your way. You have devoted significant time and effort to this workbook and have built a foundation to sustain your growth mindset. You now have had considerable practice in spotting the signs of the fixed mindset and in using the resources from this book to build a growth scaffolding to get back on the road to a life that you value. With these resources, you will recognize the fixed mindset more quickly and be able to make the shift with less difficulty. You will find that, with practice, you will be trapped in a fixed mindset less often. You will also find that the emotions of a fixed mindset will become less intense. This progress takes dedication. Remember that change can be slow but worth it. Try to stick with the strategies.

As I worked on this book, I hit the expected potholes and sometimes fell into a fixed mindset. For example, I had to deal with thinking ranging from *I am so sage and wise to write this book* to *Who am I to give all this advice?* I had to accept that this book would not be perfect and to acknowledge that attempts to make it perfect got in the way of making progress. During the editing process, I had to weather the feedback of others and worked to keep a growth mindset viewing them as resources and not judges. I had to recognize competitive comparisons—spotting emotions like envy and thoughts like *My book is so much better* and *I could never write such a terrific book!*—and shift to more constructive comparisons to improve my book. I confronted frustration and avoidance hidden by engaging in other productive activities. Even with all my knowledge about mindsets and years of studying and teaching about them, fixed mindset still happens to me. The fixed mindset is a challenge that awaits us, but with practice the shift to a growth mindset become easier and more automatic.

In summary, try not to have a fixed mindset about your growth mindset. Almost no one has a growth mindset 100 percent of the time. Almost everyone gets tripped up by life's setbacks. The process of making the shift from a fixed to a growth mindset is a lifelong undertaking. This endeavor, however, will allow you to thrive through life's expected challenges—armed with your growth mindset practices, forever stretching toward living the life you value—be it achieving your dreams, more meaningful connections, or getting closer to becoming the person you would like to be.

Acknowledgments

How do you apply sound psychological research to help people deal with tough life challenges? I was fortunate to have two mentors who guided me on this journey to answer that question, Carol S. Dweck, PhD, and Aaron T. Beck, MD. Both are inspirational in their curiosity and in their dedication to research with important real-world implications. Both changed the trajectory of my life and have made a difference in the lives of countless individuals across the globe.

More specifically I would like to thank Carol for her excitement and encouragement when I shared with her my plans to write this book. Her initial input and edits of my early chapters were invaluable in shaping the contents. I am indebted to Bob Leahy, who somehow found time to share his expertise, insights, and recommendations. I also acknowledge my New Harbinger editors, Ryan Buresh and Caleb Beckwith, an amazing team who helped me sharpen my ideas and make this book more accessible to general audiences, and my copy editor, Brady Kahn, for her diligence.

Finally my deep appreciation is extended to my personal growth mindset team: Mary Bandura, who was my first growth mindset pal during our time at the Harvard Laboratory of Human Development and shaped the concept of malleable (growth) versus fixed view of abilities in thesis conversations with Carol; my friend and colleague Diana Dill and my sister Sharon Wienstroer, who gently prodded me to write this workbook and provided insightful feedback; my daughter Katherine and my husband Alex, who gave me the space and encouragement to complete it. I am blessed to have extended family and friends who always have supported me and helped me to sustain a growth mindset through life's fixed mindset obstacles. This book is dedicated to my parents, Helen and Walter, who laid the foundations of my growth mindset.

References

Aronson, J., C. B. Fried, and C. Good. 2002. "Reducing the Effects of Stereotype Threat on African American College Students by Shaping Theories of Intelligence." *Journal of Experimental Social Psychology* 38 (2): 113–25.

Bandura, M., and C. S. Dweck. 1985. "The Relationship of Conceptions of Intelligence and Achievement Goals to Achievement-Related Cognition, Affect, and Behavior." Unpublished manuscript, Harvard University.

Beck, A. T. 1976. *Cognitive Therapy and the Emotional Disorders.* Madison, CT: International Universities Press.

Beck, A. T., A. J. Rush, B. F. Shaw, and G. Emery. 1979. *Cognitive Therapy of Depression.* New York: Guilford Press.

Beck, A. T., G. Emery, and R. L. Greenberg. 2005. *Anxiety Disorders and Phobias: A Cognitive Perspective.* 20th ed. New York: Basic Books.

Beer, J. S. 2002. "Implicit Self-Theories of Shyness." *Journal of Personality and Social Psychology* 83 (4): 1009–24.

Blackwell, L. S., K. H. Trzesniewski, and C. S. Dweck. 2007. "Implicit Theories of Intelligence Predict Achievement Across an Adolescent Transition: A Longitudinal Study and an Intervention." *Child Development* 78 (1): 246–63.

Cowan, L. 2014. "Matthew McConaughey: Finding Comfort in Uncomfortable Roles." *Sunday Morning*, February 9. CBS News. https://www.cbsnews.com/news/matthew-mcconaughey-on-dallas-buyers-club/.

Dweck, C. S. 2006. *Mindset: The New Psychology of Success.* New York: Random House.

Dweck, C. S., and E. S. Elliott-Moskwa. 2010. "Self-Theories: The Roots of Defensiveness." In *Social Psychological Foundations of Clinical Psychology*, edited by J. E. Maddux and J. P. Tangney. New York: Guilford Press.

Elliott, E. S., and C. S. Dweck. 1988. "Goals: An Approach to Motivation and Achievement." *Journal of Personality and Social Psychology* 54 (1): 5–12.

Good, C., J. Aronson, and M. Inzlicht. 2003. "Improving Adolescents' Standardized Test Performance: An Intervention to Reduce the Effects of Stereotype Threat." *Journal of Applied Developmental Psychology* 24 (6): 645–62.

Hayes, S. C., and J. Lillis. 2012. *Acceptance and Commitment Therapy.* Washington, DC: American Psychological Association.

Hofmann, S. G., A. Asnaani, I. J. Vonk, A. T. Sawyer, and A. Fang. 2012. "The Efficacy of Cognitive Behavioral Therapy: A Review of Meta-Analyses." *Cognitive Therapy and Research* 36 (5): 427–40.

Hofmann, S. G., A. T. Sawyer, A. A. Witt, and D. Oh. 2010. "The Effect of Mindfulness-Based Therapy on Anxiety and Depression: A Meta-Analytic Review." *Journal of Consulting and Clinical Psychology* 78 (2): 169–83.

Hong, Y., C. Chiu, C. S. Dweck, D. M.-S. Lin, and W. Wan. 1999. "Implicit Theories, Attributions, and Coping: A Meaning System Approach." *Journal of Personality and Social Psychology* 77 (3): 588–99.

Kammrath, L. K., and C. S. Dweck. 2006. "Voicing Conflict: Preferred Conflict Strategies Among Incremental and Entity Theorists." *Personality and Social Psychology Bulletin* 32 (11): 1497–508.

Kaplan, J. S., and D. F. Tolin. 2011. "Exposure Therapy for Anxiety Disorders." *Psychiatric Times* 28 (9). September 6. https://www.psychiatrictimes.com/view/exposure-therapy-anxiety-disorders.

Kray, L. J., and M. P. Haselhuhn. 2007. "Implicit Negotiation Beliefs and Performance: Experimental and Longitudinal Evidence." *Journal of Personality and Social Psychology* 93 (1): 49–64.

Leahy, R. L. 2004. *Contemporary Cognitive Therapy: Theory, Research, and Practice.* New York: Guilford Press.

Leahy, R. L., D. Tirch, and L. A. Napolitano. 2011. *Emotion Regulation in Psychotherapy: A Practitioner's Guide.* New York: Guilford Press.

Mangels, J. A., B. Butterfield, J. Lamb, C. Good, C. S. Dweck. 2006. "Why Do Beliefs About Intelligence Influence Learning Success? A Social Cognitive Neuroscience Model." *Social Cognitive and Affective Neuroscience* 1 (2): 75–86.

Mueller, C. M., and C. S. Dweck. 1998. "Praise for Intelligence Can Undermine Children's Motivation and Performance." *Journal of Personality and Social Psychology* 75 (1): 33–52.

Nussbaum, A. D., and C. S. Dweck. 2008. "Defensiveness Versus Remediation: Self-Theories and Modes of Self-Esteem Maintenance." *Personality and Social Psychology Bulletin* 34 (5): 599–612.

Persons, J. B., and M. A. Tompkins. 2007. "Cognitive-Behavioral Case Formulation." In *Handbook of Psychotherapy Case Formulation*, edited by T. D. Eells. New York: Guilford Press.

Robins, R. W., and J. L. Pals. 2002. "Implicit Self-Theories in the Academic Domain: Implications for Goal Orientation, Attributions, Affect, and Self-Esteem Change." *Self and Identity* 1 (4): 313–36.

Wood, R., and A. Bandura. 1989. "Impact of Conceptions of Ability on Self-Regulatory Mechanisms and Complex Decision Making." *Journal of Personality and Social Psychology* 56 (3): 407–15.

Young, J. E., J. S. Klosko, and M. E. Weishaar. 2003. *Schema Therapy: A Practitioner's Guide.* New York: Guilford Press.

Elaine Elliott-Moskwa, PhD, is a mentee of Carol S. Dweck and Aaron T. Beck, with whom she did postdoctoral work at the Harvard School of Education, and trained in cognitive behavioral therapy (CBT) at the University of Pennsylvania, respectively. She helped to establish the CBT training program at Harvard Medical School/Massachusetts General Hospital. Currently, she is president of the Academy of Cognitive and Behavioral Therapies, and has a private practice in Princeton, NJ.

Foreword writer **Carol S. Dweck, PhD**, is Lewis and Virginia Eaton Professor of Psychology at Stanford University. In addition to receiving awards for her pioneering research on fixed and growth mindsets, Dweck has been elected to the American Academy of Arts and Sciences, and the National Academy of Sciences. Her book, *Mindset*, has been widely acclaimed and translated into forty languages.

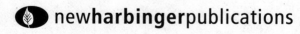

MORE BOOKS from
NEW HARBINGER PUBLICATIONS

ACT DAILY JOURNAL

Get Unstuck and Live Fully with Acceptance and Commitment Therapy

978-1684037377 / US $18.95

THE UPWARD SPIRAL

Using Neuroscience to Reverse the Course of Depression, One Small Change at a Time

978-1626251205 / US $18.95

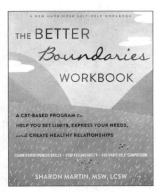

THE BETTER BOUNDARIES WORKBOOK

A CBT-Based Program to Help You Set Limits, Express Your Needs, and Create Healthy Relationships

978-1684037582 / US $24.95

THE CBT WORKBOOK FOR PERFECTIONISM

Evidence-Based Skills to Help You Let Go of Self-Criticism, Build Self-Esteem, and Find Balance

978-1684031535 / US $24.95

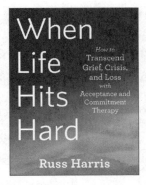

WHEN LIFE HITS HARD

How to Transcend Grief, Crisis, and Loss with Acceptance and Commitment Therapy

978-1684039012 / US $19.95

THE LITTLE BOOK OF BIG CHANGE

The No-Willpower Approach to Breaking Any Habit

978-1626252301 / US $16.95

newharbingerpublications

1-800-748-6273 / newharbinger.com

(VISA, MC, AMEX / prices subject to change without notice)

Follow Us

Did you know there are **free tools** you can download for this book?

Free tools are things like **worksheets**, **guided meditation exercises**, and **more** that will help you get the most out of your book.

You can download free tools for this book—whether you bought or borrowed it, in any format, from any source—from the New Harbinger website. All you need is a NewHarbinger.com account. Just use the URL provided in this book to view the free tools that are available for it. Then, click on the "download" button for the free tool you want, and follow the prompts that appear to log in to your NewHarbinger.com account and download the material.

You can also save the free tools for this book to your **Free Tools Library** so you can access them again anytime, just by logging in to your account! Just look for this button on the book's free tools page.

+ Save this to my free tools library

If you need help accessing or downloading free tools, visit **newharbinger.com/faq** or contact us at **customerservice@newharbinger.com**.